Carolyn S. Swallow

The Economics of Aging

The Economics of Aging

James H. Schulz

Florence Heller Graduate School
Brandeis University

Wadsworth Publishing Company, Inc.
Belmont, California

ISBN 0-534-00469-5
L.C. Cat. Card No. 76-13923
Printed in the United States of America
1 2 3 4 5 6 7 8 9 10---80 79 78 77 76

Preface

Economic destitution among the aged has been a recognized national problem for almost half a century; yet economists have virtually ignored the problem. Over the years only a handful of economists have given much attention to the economic issues associated with a growing aged population and the fact that a substantial proportion of the United States population has shifted out of the labor force.

Policy makers and the elderly themselves generally agree that economic security in old age is one of the most important problems needing solution. Yet, as in other areas of knowledge, misconceptions abound. Most aged are not poor; they are not the group most seriously hurt by inflation; they have not been *forced* to retire.

We do not know the answers to all the questions raised concerning the economic situation of the aged. However, this book attempts to present a wide range of existing knowledge, which permits a more sophisticated view of the many issues and which, in some cases, challenges the conventional wisdom.

Much of the earlier work in this area by economists and government agencies has focused on documenting the relatively poor economic status of the aged and problems associated with the social security system. Now, with dramatic declines in labor-force participation by older workers and equally dramatic, and related, increases in economic support programs for the elderly, many other major issues have arisen. Just a few of these are:

1. The economic implications of demographic shifts in the age structure of our population.
2. The structural employment problems of older workers in an economic milieu of age discrimination, rapid technological change, and frequent geographic shifts (national and international) by business.

3. The economic consequences and the distributional implications of the "early retirement" phenomenon.
4. The impact of inflation on the elderly and the development of appropriate indexing mechanisms.
5. The inter- and intra-generational equity of pension systems.
6. The impact of pensions on saving and investment.
7. The economic implications of a $200 billion private pension industry.
8. Appropriate economic policies toward the elderly in adopting public assistance and tax-reform programs.
9. How to design a quality health-delivery system without skyrocketing costs.

Fortunately, coincident with the expanding number of issues to be confronted, we have witnessed in recent years a significant rise in aging information, data, research, and programs. Our knowledge of the economic problems and alternative solutions is changing very rapidly.

To date, however, there has been no comprehensive review of what we know and where we are with regard to the economics of aging. The available knowledge and statistics are scattered in widely diverse places—many quite obscure. One major objective of this book is to bring much of this information together for the first time.

I have tried to cover a wide range of technical topics in a relatively nontechnical and concise manner. Inevitably a lot of the complexities and much of the existing literature could not be discussed. However, I have recommended at the end of each chapter the additional reading that in my judgment would be most useful for those readers seeking to extend their knowledge on particular issues. Again, however, I have tried to avoid highly technical works.

Some readers may be surprised by the proportion of the book devoted to pension issues (four chapters). To me, however, the key to understanding the current and future economic status of the aged is an understanding of private and public pension programs. Therefore, I have devoted considerable space in the book to describing these programs and, more importantly, to discussing their economic impact on the younger and older populations.

This book should be a useful supplement for students in courses dealing with the psychological and social aspects of aging. I hope it will also assist the rapidly growing number of persons involved in developing and carrying out policies and programs for the elderly—persons who often confront the economic issues of aging on a personal and daily basis. Finally, persons approaching retirement and persons assisting them in "retirement planning" should find a great deal of useful information in this book.

To the many people who read all or part of this book prior to publication and provided me with suggested changes, corrections, and useful insights, I express my sincere thanks:

Vern Bengtson, Chief, Laboratory for Social Organization and Behavior, University of Southern California;

Robert Binstock, Director, Program in the Economics and Politics of Aging, Brandeis University;

William Birdsal, School of Social Work, University of Michigan;

Colin Campbell, Professor of Economics, Dartmouth College;

Wilbur J. Cohen, Dean, School of Education, University of Michigan;

Alan Fox, Office of Research and Statistics, Social Security Administration;

Walter Kolodrubetz, Pension Benefit Guarantee Corporation;

Juanita Kreps, Vice-President and Professor of Economics, Duke University;

Donald Landay, Bureau of Labor Statistics, Department of Labor;

Patience Lauriat, Office of Research and Statistics, Social Security Administration;

Dan McGill, Chairman and Research Director, Pension Research Council, University of Pennsylvania;

Elizabeth Meier, National Institute of Industrial Gerontology, National Council on the Aging;

Harold Orbach, Department of Sociology, Kansas State University;

George Rohrlich, Professor of Economics and Social Policy, Temple University;

Charles Schottland, Professor of Law and Social Welfare, Brandeis University;

Harold Sheppard, American Institute for Research;

Alfred Skolnik, Office of Research and Statistics, Social Security Administration;

Gayle Thompson, Office of Research and Statistics, Social Security Administration;

Lawrence Thompson, Staff Economist, Office of Income Security Policy, Department of Health, Education, and Welfare;

Clark Tibbitts, Director, National Clearinghouse on Aging, Administration on Aging;

Harry Weitz, Chief, Pension Section, Statistics Canada;

Yung-Ping Chen, Department of Economics, University of California, Los Angeles.

Also, I wish to thank the Bureau of Labor Statistics, Revenue Canada Taxation, the Social Security Administration, and Statistics Canada for making various unpublished statistics available for this book. And, finally, my sincere thanks to Margaret Stubbs for her research and typing assistance.

I first became interested in the economics of aging when some years ago I had the opportunity to ask one of the most knowledgeable persons in the aging field, Clark Tibbitts, "What have economists contributed to our knowledge about growing old?" His answer and challenge to a young graduate student who was then searching for a dissertation topic—"Why don't you find out?"—triggered a sequence of events of which this book is a product. It is appropriate then that the book begins with an introduction by Clark Tibbitts, a person who has dedicated a major portion of his life to improving the social and economic welfare of older persons.

James H. Schulz
Waltham, Massachusetts

Contents

Introduction

With *The Economics of Aging* Professor James H. Schulz has made another significant contribution to understanding and disseminating knowledge relative to one of the most compelling and complex aspects of individual and societal aging. Like its predecessor, *Providing Adequate Retirement Income*,* the new book appears at a time when the issue of the proportion of national resources that should be allocated to older and retired people assumes major importance in American policy development.

The timeliness of *The Economics of Aging* is attested also by the coincidence of its appearance with a number of other significant developments. These include a surge of public awareness and concern with the circumstances of the rapidly growing older population; a nationwide interest in gerontology on the part of college and university students; the desire of personnel employed in the aging field to develop greater competencies in their work; and the rapid expansion of course offerings and curricula responsive to the demand for trained policy makers, planners, program developers and administrators, researchers, and teachers for the field.

The availability of a text dealing with the economic aspects of aging should aid materially in closing the gap in the subject matter of aging as it is usually presented. The appearance of this text provides an opportunity to acquaint students with the economic elements as an essential complement to the biomedical and psychosocial subject matter that constitutes much of the content at the present time. It may well lead to the provision of well-rounded minors and majors in gerontology.

*J. H. Schulz, G. Carrin, H. Krupp, M. Peschke, E. Sclar, J. Van Steenberge, *Providing Adequate Retirement Income* (Hanover, N.H.: New England Press for Brandeis University Press, 1974).

The basic phenomena of aging—increasing average life expectancy, larger numbers and proportions of older people in society, and vastly altered functions of older adults in societal institutions—are largely economic in origin. They are simultaneously causes and consequences of profound and rapid changes in the objectives, methods, and volume of scientific and technological advances and exponential increases in productivity. These advances are directly related to the development and use of energy and to the nature, locus, and amount of production of goods and services required to satisfy human needs and aspirations in highly developed societies. Understanding of the origins and future of aging is conditioned, to a considerable degree, by a knowledge of these forces.

The economics of aging is concerned also with a range of individual and societal phenomena, problems, and issues consequent upon the growing number and proportions of aging and aged people in the population. It includes such matters as the expenditure of time over the later stages of adulthood, particularly following the tapering off of parental and work roles; separation from the labor force; changes in amounts and sources of income and their effect on patterns of consumption including the ability to purchase health and medical care, housing, other services, and the amenities of living in an advanced society. The economics of aging also can illuminate other problems of the later years such as family and intergenerational relationships, social status, and personal and social adjustment as they are rooted in changes in income and employment status.

Societally, the allocation of national income and resources to older persons and their apportionment among such areas as health, housing, social, recreation, education, transportation come within the purview of economics. So, too, do such matters as individual versus collective responsibility for meeting needs, the effect of providing for older people on the income and availability of goods and services for younger elements of the population, the impact of large pension reserves on capital investment, the impact of social security and private pension systems on savings practices of younger adults, the relative cost and effectiveness of providing retirement income through public versus private pension systems, and the influence of pension income on the labor-force participation of older workers.

Professor Schulz deals with all of the topics mentioned to a greater or lesser degree. Approximately one-half of his book is devoted to public and private pension systems, because he believes, as he states, that they are the key to understanding the current and future economic status of the aged. He points out that our present retirement-income maintenance system or systems are still comparatively new and formative. Several issues arise from inadequate coverage of the working population (by private systems), awareness of a number of inequities, potential effects of declining fertility and a rising dependency ratio, and uncertainty as to the proper role of government in retirement financing. Because of such issues and because of the dynamic nature of the entire field, the economics of aging will require continuing intensive study and efforts at problem resolution.

The foregoing discussion points to the conclusion that knowledge of the principal economic elements of aging, particularly of income-support systems and their individual and societal ramifications, is essential preparation for those who would participate in societal decision making, is necessary as preparation for coping with the circumstances of later life, and is a condition of successful careers in many of the occupations in the gerontological field.

The economic and economic-related issues identified by Professor Schulz can be resolved successfully only through the democratic process involving all who choose to participate. It is patent that participation can be useful only if it is based on knowledge of the subject matter involved.

From the individual or personal point of view virtually every member of society has a stake in the resolution of most of the issues. Nearly all currently employed workers will leave the work force at some time, and, as the author points out, will have a period of twenty to thirty years in retirement. Thus, almost all young and middle-aged people may expect to become beneficiaries of a public and/or private pension system that will be a major determinant of their level and style of life for up to one-fourth or one-third of their lifetime.

Finally, those who are preparing for employment or who already are employed in policy development, planning, and program administration in behalf of older people will be called upon increasingly to demonstrate a systematic knowledge of aging, including the economic elements and their significance for other elements.

The author states in his preface that he has tried to cover a wide range of technical topics in a relatively nontechnical and concise manner. Teachers who elect to use the book, their students, and independent readers will be pleased to discover that Professor Schulz achieved his goal to an admirable degree.

Clark Tibbitts, Director
National Clearinghouse on Aging
Administration on Aging
U.S. Department of Health, Education, and Welfare

Chapter One

Looking Ahead to the Retirement Years

Not too many years ago it was relatively easy to write about the economic situation of the elderly population. All one needed to do was cite statistics that confirmed what everyone knew from either personal experience or observation. For years now everyone has known that most of the elderly have suffered from serious economic deprivation—that their incomes were inadequate, that inflation exacerbated the situation by reducing real incomes and eroding savings, and that the aged were one of the largest poverty groups in the country.

Today the situation is much more complex, due in large part to our nation's very positive response to the economic plight of the elderly. During the past few decades major breakthroughs have occurred in the development of private and public programs to deal with the economic problems of old age:

1. Over the past ten years, social security old-age benefits have been increased by almost 100 percent, significantly faster than inflation over the same period.
2. Private pension programs have spread throughout industry and have grown rapidly—with dramatic increases in benefit levels.
3. Public health insurance programs have been created—currently providing over $15 billion a year in benefits to older persons.
4. Property tax relief laws have been legislated in 96 percent of our states.
5. Old-age assistance has been abolished and a new Supplemental Security Income Program (SSI) has taken its place. This program roughly doubles the number of low-income elderly eligible for income supplementation. In addition, it raised benefit levels in twenty-four states above the previous levels of old-age assistance—in some cases dramatically.

1

These new programs have resulted in a large shift of income from the working population to the retired population and a significant drop in poverty among the aged. The U.S. Bureau of the Census (1976) reports that in 1974 persons age 65 and over received money income of about $92 billion. Despite sharply rising retirement rates, this represented about 10 percent of total money income for all age groups, the same percentage share as measured by the "Survey of the Aged" for 1967. (Bixby, 1970) Thus, for the first time a new question is being seriously posed: "Have we done enough for the aged?"

Some people think we have done too much. Writing in the *Washington Post*, columnist David S. Broder, for example, concluded that "the significant, semi-hidden story in the... federal budget is that America's public resources are increasingly being mortgaged for the use of a single group within our country: the elderly. The benefits being paid to them are rising faster than any other major category of federal spending, and the taxes being levied—mainly on their children—to finance those benefits are also going up faster than any others."

Have we done enough? To answer the question we can no longer generalize about the economic situation of all the aged as one group. Instead we must look at the multitude of programs for the elderly and analyze their impact on various *subgroups* of the elderly population. We must distinguish, for example, between the very old aged and those just retiring, between widowed and married women, and between those with private pensions and those with only social security.

The Right to Retire

As observed by Donahue, Orbach, and Pollak (1960), "retirement is a phenomenon of modern industrial society.... The older people of previous societies were not retired persons; there was no retirement role." A number of developments, however, changed this.

Even *before* public and private pension systems were widely established, large numbers of older persons were not in the labor force. As early as 1900, for example, almost one-third of all men age 65 and over were "retired," in large part because of health problems. Prior to the institution of pension systems, however, older persons not in the labor force had to rely on their own (often meager) resources, help from relatives, or public and private charity. Over the years recognition spread that complete reliance on these sources of old-age support was unsatisfactory. *Public pensions were, in part, a reaction to the need of more rational support mechanisms for older persons unable to work.*

Industrialization created a new problem. In contrast to the farm, where people could almost always "work" (even if it was at reduced levels), industry was characterized by a large amount of job insecurity. Recurrent recessions and depressions and shifts in employment opportunities created competition for the available jobs. *Thus, another motivation for establishing pensions was to create a mechanism that would encourage older workers to leave the work force and create jobs for younger workers.*

But probably most important of all, industrial growth—fueled by rapid technological change—resulted in vast increases in economic output. As we discuss at length in Chapter 3, economic growth provides an expanding option for greater leisure with a simultaneous increase in living standards. That is, *the rapid economic growth of the twentieth century made it possible to more easily support older people who could not (or did not wish to) work.* Retirement became economically feasible.

Thus, we see the institutionalization of retirement arising as a result of and reaction to (a) the needs of large numbers of elderly unable to work, (b) short-run fluctuations in employment opportunities for both the young and the old, and (c) expanding economic resources over the long run. Pension programs were developed that "provided compensation based upon years of service rather than upon need per se. They were to emerge as an 'earned right' and were to become instrumental in defining a retirement status as appropriate for the older worker." (Friedman and Orbach, 1974)

Changing Expectations

As just indicated, until recently retirement meant dependency—dependency on relatives, friends, private charity, or government welfare. Indications are that many elderly tended to accept a subsistence lifestyle as the best that could be expected in old age. Attitudinal surveys have found, for example, that despite their relatively low economic status, very *high* proportions of the elderly viewed their economic situations as satisfactory and not below their expectations.*

Predictably, those *approaching* old age viewed the period negatively. "The widespread opposition to retirement reported in studies during the 1940's and the early 1950's reflected an overwhelming concern over the consequences of serious deprivation associated with retirement that this had established." (Friedman and Orbach, 1974)

*See, for example, the report of Louis Harris and Associates listed in the Suggested Readings at the end of this chapter.

Retirement expectations are changing, however. In part, this has resulted from increases in living standards at all ages. More importantly, the development of pension programs and the continuous improvement in their provisions have given the elderly increasing independence and for the first time placed a comfortable standard of living within the reach of many. Increasing pension benefits and pension coverage seem to stimulate demands for still higher retirement incomes.

Aging Populations

At the same time that retirement-income expectations are changing, we are witnessing an aging of populations around the world. This phenomenon is relatively recent and restricted to a small but growing group of countries.

Table 1 shows the proportion of the population over age 59 and age 65. Using a classification scheme developed by Rosset (1964), nations with 8 percent or more of their population over the age of 64 are classified as "aging populations." Most of the countries in Table 1 have populations meeting the 8 percent criteria, with almost half of them having percentages greater than 12 percent.

In the United States, levels of fertility have been declining over a period of many years. As a result, population growth has slowed, and there is a real possibility of reaching zero population growth conditions in the not too distant future.* Rejda and Shepler (1973), studying the impact of lower birthrates on social security costs, warn of an increasing financial burden facing future active workers. Table 2 shows projected shifts in the age distribution of the population if the nation approaches zero population growth. The ratio of age 65 and over persons to those age 20–64 is projected to rise from 19 percent in 1970 to about 28 percent in the year 2050.

Given this aging trend, many people are concerned about the increased competition that they anticipate will arise among different age groups as each strives for larger shares of the nation's output. For example, improving retirement income by increasing social security often heads the list of demands by the aged segment of the population; in contrast, this is a relatively unimportant priority for younger workers.

Given the various mechanisms for retirement-income provision—social security, public assistance, private insurance, private charity, and/or personal savings—the fundamental economic fact

*Demographic developments are much more complex than our brief comments might suggest. For a good discussion of the various issues see Cutler and Harootyan (1975).

Table 1   Aged Populations in Various Countries
(Percent)

	Year	Percent Age 60 and Over	Percent Age 65 and Over
Australia	1971	12.3	8.3
Austria	1971	20.2	14.2
Belgium	1968[a]	18.8	13.1
Canada	1966	11.0	7.7
Democratic Republic of Germany	1971	22.1	15.6
Denmark	1968[a]	17.0	11.9
England/Wales	1971	19.2	13.3
Federal Republic of Germany	1970	20.0	NA[b]
Finland	1970	14.4	9.4
France	1968	18.8	13.4
Greece	1971	21.1	10.3
Ireland	1971	15.6	11.1
Italy	1968[a]	15.2	10.3
Japan	1970	10.6	7.1
Netherlands	1971	14.6	10.3
Northern Ireland	1970[a]	14.4	10.0
Norway	1969[a]	18.0	12.8
Portugal	1969[a]	12.8	8.8
Scotland	1971	17.9	12.3
Spain	1970	14.1	9.7
Sweden	1970	19.9	13.9
Switzerland	1970	16.4	11.4
United States	1974[a]	14.6	10.3
U.S.S.R.	1970	11.8	NA[b]
Yugoslavia	1971	12.2	7.9

Sources: United Nations, *Demographic Yearbook* (New York: United Nations, 1971, 1973, 1974); United States Bureau of the Census, *Current Population Reports*, Series P-25, No. 529, "Estimates of the Population of the United States, by Age, Sex, and Race: July 1, 1974 and April 1, 1970" (Washington, D.C.: U.S. Government Printing Office, 1974); *1973 Year Book of Labour Statistics* (Geneva: International Labour Office, 1973).
[a]Estimated.
[b]Not available.

remains that the part of national output consumed in any particular year by those *retired* is produced by the *working* population, regardless of the mix of mechanisms employed. Figure 1 shows, for example, the proportion of total output estimated to be consumed by the aged in 1974. Some of this output was produced by persons over age 64 still in the labor force. But most of the aged, consuming about 10 percent of total output, did not participate in the production process.

Table 2 The Changing United States Age Distribution: Moving to a Stationary State Under Zero Population Growth Conditions

Category	1970	1985	2000	2025	2050	Ultimate Stationary
Ages 0–19 (Thousands)	77,150	76,228	78,359	78,225	78,088	77,848
Ages 20–64 (Thousands)	107,497	131,675	149,335	162,355	163,853	163,993
Ages 65 and Over (Thousands)	20,156	25,274	28,052	42,442	46,074	46,213
Total Population (Thousands)	204,800	233,179	255,747	283,021	288,016	288,112
Percent of Population Age 65 and Over	9.8	10.8	11.0	15.0	16.0	16.0
Ratio of Age 65 and Over to Ages 20–64	.188	.192	.188	.261	.281	.282
Percent of Ratio Over 1970 Ratio	100	102	100	139	149	150
Median Age in Years	27.9	30.1	33.4	36.7	37.3	37.3

Source: George E. Rejda and Richard J. Shepler, "The Impact of Zero Population Growth on the OASDHI Program," *The Journal of Risk and Insurance* 40 (September 1973), Table 1; compiled by Rejda and Shepler from data in U.S. Bureau of the Census, *Current Population Reports*, Series P-25, No. 480, "Illustrative Population Projections for the United States: The Demographic Effects of Alternate Paths to Zero Growth" (Washington, D.C.: U.S. Government Printing Office, 1972).

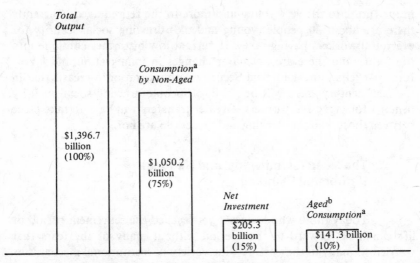

a Includes government non-transfer expenditures apportioned on a per capita basis between aged and non-aged.

b Persons age 65 or more.

Figure 1. Consumption and Investment of National Output in 1974
Source: Estimated using data in *Economic Report of the President* (Washington, D.C.: U.S. Government Printing Office, 1975).

It has been pointed out by some observers, however, that the rising costs of benefits to the retired are offset to some degree by the declining costs of educating children (given lower birthrates). Using the data in Table 2, for example, we can calculate the proportion that persons age 0–19 and age 65 or more represent of the total population (often called the "dependency ratio"). In 1970 this proportion was 48 percent. Surprisingly—despite the rise in the percentage of aged in the population—the dependency ratio is projected to *fall* by the year 2050 to about 43 percent, given the small increase in the numbers of those under age 20.

The projected fall in the dependency ratio indicates that we should give attention to the changing numbers of *both* young and old. Unfortunately, the extent to which the *reduced costs* of fewer children might offset the *rising costs* of more retired persons has not yet been systematically studied.

In any event, it is clear that we need to have institutional or cultural devices that permit (and facilitate) some part of the working population's output being available to those not working—less perhaps in the future to the very young and more to the retired aged. Currently there are about 30 people (young and old) drawing social security for every 100 workers paying taxes. If current low birthrates continue into the future and there are no major changes in immigration and labor-force participation, the Social Security Administration forecasts that in the next century there will be about 50 people drawing social security benefits for every 100 workers. Greater transfers will have to take place between those who are working and those who are not.

The Need for Individual and National Retirement Planning

Today those who have not yet reached the retirement period of life can look forward to that period without many of the fears that worried so many in the past. A wide variety of institutional mechanisms are now available to help individuals provide for their economic needs. In fact, almost all individuals *are required* to make substantial provision for retirement by mandatory participation in social security and other pension programs.

With the emergence of retirement as a normative expectation and the development of a variety of institutional arrangements affecting the terms and conditions of retirement, the economics of aging takes on a different perspective. As we shall see in the chapters to follow, the level of retirement living has generally improved but is still subject to a large degree of variation and also individual discretion. More importantly, however, the level and adequacy of retirement living are influenced by the many uncertainties and risks that are associated with the institutional mechanisms we have created. Savings opportunities completely secure from the risks of inflation are generally not available. Private pension coverage varies greatly among industries and occupations, and job change may mean the loss of some or all of these pension rights. The ultimate level of social security benefits can be severely reduced by the misfortunes of structural unemployment or illness and by the obligations of child-care—all of which keep individuals out of the regular labor force for long periods.

People can and should begin to look forward to the challenges and opportunities of retirement. But there is still a major need for individuals to think about and plan for retirement. In this book we look at various economic aspects of that planning. The concurrent rise in (a) the level of benefits to the aged, (b) retirement expectations, and (c) the number of aged as a proportion of the population also generates a need for more *national* planning in the area of the economics of aging.

In the chapters to follow we will look at the retirement preparation problem, both from an individual and national standpoint. We begin with chapters concerned with the economic status of the current elderly and the special problems of older workers. We then discuss the nature and magnitude of the economic retirement preparation task. Finally, the concluding chapters of the book discuss private and public pensions and the special and major role they play in providing income in retirement.

Suggested Readings

Friedman, Eugene A., and Harold L. Orbach. "Adjustment to Retirement." In Silvano Arieti, ed., *The Foundations of Psychiatry*. Vol. 1, *American Handbook of Psychiatry*, 2nd ed. New York: Basic Books, 1974, pp. 609–647.
   The authors discuss the emergence and institutionalization of retirement. They also provide a comprehensive review of research on the issue of adjustment to retirement. The authors conclude that most persons today have a generally positive attitude toward retirement as a future status and that as a separate sphere of life activity, work for most workers does not seem to take precedence over other life areas.

Harris, Louis, and Associates. *The Myth and Reality of Aging in America*. Washington, D.C.: The National Council on the Aging, 1975.
   A report on a representative national sample of 4254 persons 18 years and over conducted in 1974. Topics covered are (a) public attitudes toward old age, (b) the public's image of "most" people over 65, (c) perceived social and economic contributions of the aged, (d) preparation for old age, (e) being old, (f) access to facilities, (g) the media's portrayal of the aged, and (h) the politics of old age.

Streib, G. F., and C. J. Schneider (S.J.). *Retirement in American Society: Impact and Process*. Ithaca, N.Y.: Cornell University Press, 1971.
   A longitudinal study of retirement that reports positive attitudes to retirement and satisfactory adjustments to this period of life for the majority surveyed.

U.S. Bureau of the Census. *Some Demographic Aspects of Aging in the United States*. Current Population Reports Series P-23, No. 43. Washington, D.C.: U.S. Government Printing Office, 1973.
   Discussion of the size and characteristics of the aged population over the period 1900 to 2020.

Chapter Two

The Economic Status
of the Aged

Prior to the 1960's there were relatively few data available to analyze the economic situation of the aged population in the United States. This situation changed dramatically in the early sixties as a result of the Social Security Administration's very comprehensive survey of the aged in 1962.* Since then a wide range of statistics has been published by the Social Security Administration, the Census Bureau, the Administration on Aging, the Department of Labor, and various private organizations. These data provide a variety of information on various aspects of the elderly's financial status.

Because it takes time to collect, check, analyze, and publish statistics, there is often a considerable lag in the availability of information. Since you will want to evaluate newer data as they appear, we focus in this chapter on some general concepts and problems that you need to know about to interpret the various kinds of published data. Throughout the chapter, however, we have presented illustrative statistics, the latest that were available at the time of writing. Moreover, a socioeconomic profile of the aged is presented in an appendix at the end of the chapter and includes additional data and presents some historical trends.

All statistical information is subject to great abuse; unless users are very careful, they may misinterpret or misuse the available data. The discussion below, therefore, attempts to answer two questions: What are the most useful kinds of data for evaluating the economic status of the aged, and what are the major problems in interpreting the data available?

*Known as the "1963 Survey of the Aged," the many special reports resulting from this survey were ultimately published in one volume: Epstein and Murray (1967).

Measuring the Distribution of Aged Income

While most of the available data are for *all* the aged, the most useful type of data—for analysis and evaluation purposes—are data that break down the aged population into small subgroups. Perhaps the most frequently used economic data on the elderly are from the National Census and the Current Population Survey (CPS). Unfortunately, many of these data available in published form do not show the many differences existing among the elderly.

The CPS, for example, annually surveys a national sample of the population to obtain, among other things, income information. Table 3 presents the published information for all aged persons in 1974. What writers and analysts often do is give the CPS means or medians for all or large groups of the aged. Such statistics tell us very little. Lumping all the aged population together seriously distorts the reality of the situation (in this case the economic reality). We see in Table 3, for example, the wide divergence of income among the aged and between, say, men and women.

This aggregation problem is similar to the one resulting from grouping all the aged together to generalize in terms of "their" social problems. Most people who study old age and the process of aging (gerontology) are familiar with this problem in the social and psychological areas. There is no such thing as the collectivity of the aged; the aged are a heterogeneous collection of people as diverse as the population itself. The reader should remember that this point is just as true for economic issues as it is for others.

If one views the aged as one similar group there is a tendency to try to develop for them *the* appropriate economic policy—just as in other areas we have tried to develop *the* appropriate housing policy and *the* appropriate health policy. We have learned over the years that such attempts almost always fail in diverse groups such as the aged.

The Retired Versus the Nonretired   Distributional data shown in Table 3 are more representative than just means or medians, but still hide many differences. The first step one can take toward further disaggregation of the data is very simple: Separate the aged into at least two broad categories—the retired and nonretired aged. Unfortunately, most of the data sources do not or cannot provide such a breakdown. They "do not" because often it simply does not occur to those presenting the data that it is important to make this distinction. They "cannot" because the questions asked in the survey providing the data do not always include the necessary information for judging whether a person is retired

Table 3   1974 Total Money Income of Persons 65 and Over, by Sex

Total Money Income	Men	Women
Median	$4535	$2375
Mean	$6466	$3233
Less Than $1000	1.7	7.9
$1000–1999	9.3	30.6
$2000–2999	16.7	26.9
$3000–3999	15.5	12.6
$4000–4999	12.5	6.9
$5000–5999	9.4	4.1
$6000–6999	7.1	3.1
$7000–9999	13.0	4.2
$10,000–14,999	8.1	2.5
$15,000–24,999	4.2	.9
$25,000 and Over	2.4	.2
Total Percent	100.0[a]	100.0

Source: U.S. Bureau of the Census, *Consumer Income,* Current Population Reports Series P-60, No. 99 (Washington, D.C.: U.S. Government Printing Office, 1975).
[a]Totals may not add up to 100.0 due to rounding.

or not. The result is that one sees data where the wage earners among the aged are grouped together with the non–wage earners. The earners, of course, tend to have much higher and, in most cases, adequate incomes. When they are averaged together with the non–wage earners the total mean and median income for "the aged" is increased and makes the situation look much better than it actually is for retired people and much worse than it actually is for the employed.

If one wants to segregate the retired from the nonretired, one immediately runs into the problem of how to define, for statistical purposes, being retired. Many aged persons work to supplement their pension and other retirement income. Is a person who is working twenty hours a week counted as a retired person or is he or she "partially retired"? If the latter, what does that mean?

Thus, even if one wants to divide the aged population on the basis of retirement, it is not clear whether there should be two categories or more than two. A three-category tabulation, for example, might be: full-time workers, part-time and unemployed workers, and the fully retired. In general, most discussions of the economic status of the aged do not even attempt to deal with this problem when presenting data. This omission is unfortunate since (as we will show below) this is such an important issue in evaluating the economic well-being of elderly people.

One of the few sets of *published* data that distinguished between workers and nonworkers was the Social Security Administration's 1968

Survey of the Aged. Table 4 shows the differences in the distribution of income for aged couples and nonmarried persons when two, one, and zero persons worked. The distributions for working units are much higher. For example, about half of "working couples" in 1967 had incomes over $5000, whereas about 10 percent of nonworking couples had income over that amount.

Unpublished data provided by the Social Security Administration for 1971 are also shown in Table 4. While the income levels have improved greatly between 1967 and 1971, the differences between those working and those not working remain.

In recent years, the Census Bureau has begun to publish some data giving income by employment status. Although these tabulations are less differentiated than the social security data, they provide more recent information. Table 5 shows income by employment status for 1973.

The data shown in both Tables 4 and 5 are not tabulated by "hours worked"; hence, it is impossible to distinguish between people working part- versus full-time. As we pointed out above, such information on aged incomes would be very useful.*

Different Age Groups   A second major point in analyzing data on the aged is that it often does not seem appropriate to group people together who differ in age by as much as fifteen or twenty years. When one looks at most statistics on the economic status of aged people, all persons age 65 and over are often grouped together (for example, Table 3). Again, if one tries to draw conclusions from such data one is going to be misled. To begin with it is important to note that the needs of people at these two extremes of the retirement period are often quite different. For example, we do know that the "very old" tend to have expenditure patterns that are significantly different from people who have just retired, particularly in the areas of health care, recreation, clothing, and food.

If one wants to develop a budget for the aged, then, it is probably better to develop different budgets for at least two age groups of the elderly (even though the range of ages chosen must be somewhat arbitrary). Not that you cannot find aged persons 85 and 90 years old who are as active and vigorous as someone 65 (or maybe 25). But on average there seem to be enough distinctions for analytical purposes to warrant taking a range of ages into account in the presentation and analysis of economic data.

*The 1968 Survey of the Aged data were tabulated (but not presented here) by whether or not survey units were receiving social security, which is one crude way of separating the partly from the fully retired.

Table 4 Aged Income Distribution by Work Experience, 1967

| | Married Couples | | | | | | Nonmarried Persons | | | |
| | Both Worked | | One Worked | | Neither Worked | | Worked | | Did Not Work | |
Total Money Income	1967	1971	1967	1971	1967ᵃ	1976	1967ᵃ	1971	1967	1971
Less Than $2000	10	4	11	6	30	11	42	22	80	58
$2000–4999	32	21	47	31	60	55	43	44	18	35
$5000–9999	42	36	35	38	9	27	13	22	2	5
$10,000–14,999	9	20	4	14	1	4	2	6	–ᵇ	1
$15,000 or More	6	19	3	11	1	2	1	4	–ᵇ	1
Total Percent	100ᶜ	100	100	100	100	100	100	100	100	100

Source: Data for 1967 from Lenore E. Bixby, et al., *Demographic and Economic Characteristics of the Aged* (Washington, D.C.: U.S. Government Printing Office, 1975), Table 2.8. Data for 1971 are unpublished data provided by the Social Security Administration from the March 1972 Current Population Survey.

ᵃCouples with head 65 or older and nonmarried persons 65 or over.

ᵇLess than 0.5.

ᶜTotals may not add up to 100 due to rounding.

Table 5   Money Income of Aged Households by Employment Status of Head,[a] 1973

Income	Head Not in Labor Force	Head in Labor Force
Less Than $2000	15.9	4.3
$2000–3999	32.5	17.0
$4000–6999	19.8	17.8
$7000–7999	10.5	13.7
$8000–11,999	10.4	18.1
$12,000–24,999	9.0	22.3
$25,000 or More	1.8	6.8
Total Percent	100.0[b]	100.0

Source: Derived from data in U.S. Bureau of the Census, *Consumer Income*, Current Population Reports Series P-60, No. 96 (Washington, D.C.: U.S. Government Printing Office, 1974).
[a]Heads of households (including unrelated individual in one-person households) who are age 65 or more.
[b]May not add up to 100 due to rounding.

Another reason why the aged should be separated into various age groups is that the accustomed standard of living for the *very* old versus the *newly* old is usually quite different. Each group grew up and worked during dissimilar periods. Each group's final earnings and the resulting levels of living prior to retirement are different, and, given the lengths of time involved, these differences can be quite substantial. Thus, if one is trying to evaluate the adequacy of the income for aged people, one may, on the one hand, want to take into account the fact that the *very* old themselves may have lower living-standard expectations than other aged persons who retire a decade or two later.

On the other hand, there is another factor that works in the opposite direction. When one gets very old the incidence of exceptionally high expenditures for chronic illness and institutionalization rises dramatically. For those elderly persons who experience these problems economic need can rise catastrophically.

A third point is that the incomes of those who have recently retired are often much better than those who have been retired a long time. This results mainly from the fact that the former group's earnings are typically higher and pensions based upon them are consequently better. Also, the newer retirees are more likely to reap gains from the recent establishment of a private pension or improvements in an old plan.

Finally—especially given the rise in so-called early retirement in the United States—it becomes increasingly unsatisfactory to talk about only those people aged 65 and older as being aged. We know that designating people at some chronological age such as 65 as being "old" is a very unsatisfactory way of approaching the question of who the aged are. It is unsatisfactory from a physical standpoint, from a mental capacity standpoint, from a social involvement standpoint, and from many other viewpoints. We know that people age differently in terms of various characteristics.

The more serious economic problems of aging commonly arise or are aggravated by the cessation of earnings following retirement. Thus, one part of the aged population that is important to study from an economic standpoint is the one that has the most economic problems—those families where there are no regular workers. Increasingly this group includes people who are less than 65 years of age. If we look at the persons younger than age 65, we can logically divide them into two groups: those younger than age 62 and those age 62 to 64. Age 62 seems to be an appropriate dividing point since it is at age 62 that initial social security eligibility begins for everyone except widows (who can qualify at age 60).

Persons who retire before age 62 must rely on private pensions and/or their own assets and income from these assets. Data indicate that this latter group tends to be composed of both very high-income people and very low-income people (with very few in the middle). That is, we find among this very early retirement group those people who *have* to retire early even though they do not have enough money and those people who *can* retire very early because they have sufficient economic resources to live satisfactorily.

The age 62–64 group, normally referred to as the "early retirement group," receives reduced social security benefits. Ever since the early retirement provisions under social security were first introduced (in 1956 for women and 1961 for men), more than half of the men and women starting to receive social security old-age retirement benefits have opted for reduced benefits before age 65. The Social Security Administration reports in its 1973 *Annual Statistical Supplement* that, for example, 54 percent of the men and 70 percent of the women workers who *began* receiving social security old-age benefits received *reduced* benefits.

Again, actual published economic data on various age groupings of the elderly population are sparse. Table 6 presents data from the 1968 Survey of the Aged that illustrate the income differences between age groups by looking at young versus very old nonmarried aged persons.

What Survey Unit? Still another problem in evaluating the economic status of the elderly (a problem common to all survey tabulations of income distribution) is defining the household unit to be

Table 6 Nonmarried Aged: Income Distribution by Age, 1967

Total Money Income	Age			
	65–69	70–74	75–79	80 and Over
Less than $1000	14	15	21	39
$1000–2499	36	46	50	45
$2500–4999	26	28	20	12
$5000–9999	19	10	7	3
$10,000–14,999	3	1	1	1
$15,000 and Over	2	1	1	—a
Total Percent	100	100	100	100

Source: Lenore E. Bixby, *Demographic and Economic Characteristics of the Aged* (Washington, D.C.: U.S. Government Printing Office, 1975).
aLess than 0.5.

used in the survey. Any survey or census must define the household unit that will be the basis for reporting the findings.

The household unit varies from survey to survey. The Social Security Administration defines "aged units" as (a) married couples living together with one or both members over a specified age (60 or 65), and (b) nonmarried individuals who are over the specified age or married persons living apart from their spouses. The Bureau of the Census defines "aged families" as a group of two or more persons related by blood, marriage, or adoption and residing together with a family head over age 64 and "unrelated aged individuals" as persons *not* living with any relatives (alone or in a household). It is very important that one be aware of such differences when comparing various surveys.

One needs to find out just what the survey unit is and the extent to which there is comparability between different surveys. In 1971, for example, the Census Bureau reported that 12 percent of the individuals in aged *families* had poverty incomes, while the Social Security Administration reported 14 percent of aged *couples* with poverty level incomes. And for the same year the poverty rate for *unrelated individuals* was 42 percent versus 50 percent for *nonmarried individuals*.

If an aged person(s) lives with his children or if the children live with their aged parent(s), should the two "units" be reported separately or should the income be lumped together into one big "family"? It often makes a significant difference in the final results that are reported. There is a tendency to combine all the incomes of people "living together." The result has been that a lot of aged poverty in the past has been hidden because the poorest aged—those who are unable to live by themselves—were submerged into the bigger and usually more prosperous family unit.

One might argue that if the aged are living with a family unit and the family unit is not itself poor then the aged standard of living is not likely to be poor. Using this perspective, one can argue further that there is no problem in such cases and that if you statistically separate the aged out (perhaps to try to justify higher pension benefits) you are basing the analysis on an artificial and very unreal situation.

The opposing view, however, is that many of these people are not necessarily treated as "members" of the family. They are there by necessity, and often families do not permit them to share fully in the higher standard of living of the rest of the family. Or, even if the younger members of the family want them to share fully, many aged people are too independent to be willing to draw heavily upon the resources of the rest of the family. They would rather—even though they live within the family—live at a lower, perhaps subsistence, level.

Historically we know that as social security benefit levels have increased many aged persons have moved out of these families at the first opportunity and set up independent households. Statistically, as a result of this process of family units breaking up, these new units headed by an aged person show up in the data (previously submerged in another household unit). Since these new aged units almost always have very low income, the process tends to increase the reported incidence of poverty among the aged.

We find, for example, that during certain periods the number of persons in poverty has declined among nonaged groups but has risen among the aged (partly as a result of the separation of the aged out of other families).

Thus, when the statistics show aged poverty increasing, it is not necessarily true that the situation is actually getting worse. In part the statistics are a reflection of things getting better. As pension benefits go up, some of the poor aged who prefer independent living are able to break out of other family units and thus become identifiable statistical units.* But, as discussed above, it can be argued that they were always poor, and all that has changed is their living arrangements.

Socioeconomic Differences Differentiation of the aged population by various socioeconomic characteristics must also be made. Table 7, for example, shows the differences in 1974 money income for persons age 62 and over by race and marital status. We see that the differences are quite large.

---

*Rising income (such as larger pensions) also makes it possible for some aged who would have otherwise been forced to live with relatives out of economic necessity to avoid entirely this situation and hence always to be an identifiable statistical unit.

Table 7   1974 Total Money Income of Persons 62 Years Old and Over, by Race

| | Married Couples | | Single, Widowed, or Divorced | |
Income Class	White	Black	White	Black
Less Than $3000	7.6	20.5	50.2	77.6
$3000–4999	18.2	33.2	24.2	13.7
$5000–9999	38.2	32.1	18.0	7.7
$10,000 or More	36.0	14.2	7.7	.9
Total Percent	100.0[a]	100.0	100.0	100.0

Source: Derived from Table 54, U.S. Bureau of the Census, *Consumer Income*, Current Population Reports Series P-60, No. 101 (Washington, D.C.: U.S. Government Printing Office, 1976).
[a]May not add up to 100 due to rounding.

A recent study by the Social Security Administration of differences in social security benefits by race offers another type of data. This study shows that average nonwhite social security retirement benefits have been 25 percent less than average white benefits over the past 15 years. (Thompson, 1975)

Taxation   A final point is that most income-distribution statistics look at the pretax distribution of income. The aged, while they share in the tax advantages of the general population, also have their own special loopholes to reduce the amount of taxes they must pay. The most important of these exemptions is the nontaxation of social security benefits (earlier payments into the social security fund while working are treated as taxable income). Also important is the special provision that permits persons over age 65 to double their personal exemption amount. Finally, property-tax reductions are granted in almost all of the states for elderly persons who meet some combination of an income/assets test.

These favorable tax laws for the elderly—particularly the double exemption—tend to help the higher-income elderly more than those with low income. Stanley Surrey has estimated that nearly half of the federal tax assistance goes to individuals with incomes above $10,000. (Surrey, 1973)

After-tax data are rarely published. Both the Social Security Administration and Census Bureau data are for money income *before* taxes. Pechman and Okner, in one of the few studies of its kind available, estimate effective tax rates for 1966. Table 8 shows the tax rates for various income groups classified by the age of the family head. The 1966

Table 8   Effective Combined Federal, State, and Local Tax Rate[a] for the Nonaged and Aged, 1966

(Percent)

Family's Rank from Lowest to Highest Income	Family Head	
	Under Age 65	Age 65 or Older
Lowest Tenth[b]	29.1	26.1
Second Tenth	26.0	23.4
Third Tenth	26.7	24.5
Fourth Tenth	26.2	24.1
Fifth Tenth	26.0	24.6
Sixth Tenth	25.8	24.1
Seventh Tenth	25.5	25.3
Eighth Tenth	25.6	25.1
Ninth Tenth	25.2	24.1
Highest Tenth	25.5	27.5

Source: Joseph A. Pechman and Benjamin A. Okner, *Who Bears the Tax Burden?* (Washington, D.C.: The Brookings Institution, © 1974), Table 5-5.
[a]Assumes corporate income and property taxes are passed on at least in part to consumers.
[b]Includes only units in the sixth to tenth percentiles.
[c]Table 5-5.

combined federal, state, and local tax rates were quite similar across the income spectrum, with the rates for both the lowest and the highest income families in both age groups being slightly higher. The tax rates for the elderly are lower for all income groups except the highest.

Pechman and Okner point out, however, that the results of this type of analysis are quite sensitive to the assumptions made with regard to who actually pays various taxes, especially the corporate income and property taxes. While the tax rates remain similar for most income groups when alternative assumptions are used, this is not true for the highest and lowest groups. If it is assumed, for example, that corporate income and property taxes are paid by the owners of capital, Pechman and Okner find that the overall effective tax rate increases with income (i.e., is progressive).

In-Kind Income and Wealth

Quite obviously the money income of the aged is not a complete measure of their economic status. One has to also take into account the wealth of the aged and nonmoney benefits that are called income *in kind*. In-kind income is a way of taking into account such things as Medicare and Medicaid health benefits—services available to the aged that permit them to receive medical care without expenditure of money or at least without making expenditures equal to the market value of these medical services. Another example of in-kind income is subsidized housing. As a result of various special housing programs for the elderly, some aged persons pay for housing at a rate that is below the normal market price for such housing—a subsidy paid for by the government.

According to the Congressional Research Service (see the Suggested Readings), there are 42 major federal programs benefiting the elderly over and above those providing direct money income. The largest expenditures are for health care. The establishment of federal health insurance for the aged and disabled by amendment of the Social Security Act in 1965 resulted in a sharp decline in health expenses financed directly by the elderly. In 1966 persons age 65 and over financed about 70 percent of their health care costs by either direct payment or private health insurance. In 1974, primarily as a result of Medicare, they financed about 40 percent of these costs that way—with federal and state government expenditures rising from about $2.5 billion in 1966 to $16 billion in 1974. Figure 2 show, for example, per capita expenditures for health care costs made by other than the individual (i.e., third-party payments) in 1974 versus 1966. The trend historically has been for these in-kind benefits to the elderly to increase.

Certainly the introduction of Medicare made a significant improvement in the economic status of the elderly. It is very difficult, however, to measure this income and to incorporate it into the statistics measuring the economic status of the elderly. Some aged have very low money incomes and *high* in-kind incomes, but other aged with low incomes have only very low in-kind incomes. Looking at money income alone gives a distorted picture of the real situation.

The same situation arises with regard to assets. Most assets can be sold and thereby converted to money that can be used to buy goods and services. But one should distinguish between liquid assets and nonliquid assets. Fortunately, most published statistics on assets do make such a distinction.

Liquid assets are relatively easily converted into goods and services or money (the most liquid of assets). Liquid assets consist generally of cash, bank deposits, and corporate stocks and bonds. *Nonliquid assets* usually require more time to convert. The two major types of nonliquid assets are equity in housing and equity in a business.

Assets are held by individuals because they perform a number of very useful economic functions. Assets (or savings) are used as a precaution against unexpected happenings in the future. One puts money aside so that it can be drawn upon should the need arise. This saving

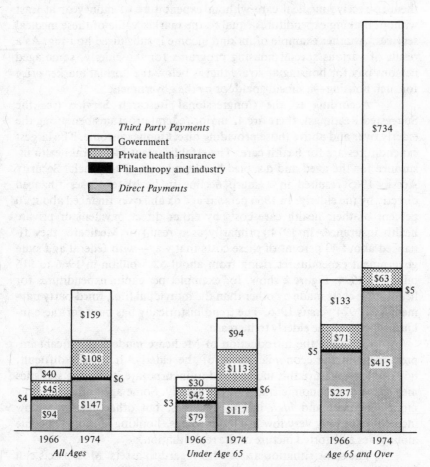

Third Party Payments
☐ Government
▨ Private health insurance
■ Philanthropy and industry
☐ *Direct Payments*

Figure 2.   Per Capita Expenditures for Health-Care Costs
Made by Third-Party Payments, 1974 Versus 1966
Source: *Social Security Bulletin, Errata,* June 1975.

might be viewed as self-insurance. Alternatively, assets are also accumulated in anticipation of known or planned large expenditures in the future; for example, because of a worsening illness one might anticipate going into a nursing home, or one might save in order to take a round-the-world retirement cruise. Still another reason for saving is to leave a legacy—passing on money to one's children or other people.

One of the most important reasons for saving is to smooth out the irregularities in the flow of income coming to an individual over his lifetime. People are becoming increasingly aware of the fact that (given current life expectancies) there is often a ten- to thirty-year period of living in retirement after earnings from work have stopped. Thus, individuals must decide how to deal financially with this nonwork period of life and whether to provide through asset accumulation economic resources to supplement pension income.

However, assets put aside as a precautionary measure or for anticipated major expenditures in old age are not available for meeting day-to-day needs. If you are worried, for example, about having high medical expenses that Medicare will not completely take care of, if you expect that you might have to go into a nursing home, or if you anticipate that property taxes will increase dramatically in your area, you must accumulate additional assets to provide for daily living.

Similarly, if you have nonliquid assets such as housing, as long as you are determined to keep that housing and not sell the property, that asset is not convertible into income to be used for day-to-day living. In effect the asset is "locked in."

In fact, a high proportion of older people (about half) own a home or have an equity in it. Thus we find that many older people have a sizable asset accumulation, but most of it is often not available for day-to-day living expenses.

We currently have few financial mechanisms that permit people to sell the equity in their home, get back money over a period of time, and still be able to live in the house. There have been proposals advanced as to how this could be done, but thus far no private organization or government has tried them out.

Thus, we must be cautious in drawing conclusions based on statistics giving the total assets of the aged population. The asset situation of some aged persons makes their economic situation appear "very good." It is often suggested that such assets should be prorated over the remaining expected lifetime of aged persons and added to income when assessing their general status and needs. This can and, in fact, has been done. (Epstein and Murray, 1967 and Weisbrod and Hansen, 1968) But the question arises as to how valid such a measure is—given precautionary considerations and the nonliquid nature of most of these assets.

Economists are correct in saying that if you totally neglect assets in assessing the economic status of the aged, you are really biasing your assessment of the economic situation of the aged. Many national leaders, when they advocate improvements for the aged, conveniently forget about these assets—allowing matters to look worse than they really are.

Yet, some studies (the most important ones by the Social Security Administration's Office of Research and Statistics) have found that prorating assets of the aged does not significantly improve the economic situation for many aged—especially those who are poor. There is a not insignificant minority of the aged for whom assets are important, but for most, taking assets into account does not make a great deal of difference. Moreover, if one looks just at the *liquid* assets of the aged, one finds that prorating these assets significantly improves the economic status of even fewer older persons.

Surveys to determine asset holdings of individuals have been undertaken very infrequently in the United States. When undertaken, asset surveys have been plagued by the problem that many people surveyed underreport their assets. Although surveys gathering information on the amounts and kinds of *income* also have underreporting problems, the amount of underreporting is greater when attempting to ascertain *assets*.

The most recent comprehensive information on the assets of the elderly is almost a decade old. The 1968 Social Security Survey of the Aged presents detailed information on the assets of the elderly in 1967. Table 9 shows the proportion of elderly units holding various amounts of financial assets and equity in owned homes. What is most striking about the information in Table 9 is the large number of older families with rel-

Table 9   Aged[a] Financial Assets and Homeowner Equity, 1967[b]

| Asset Amount | Financial Assets Only | | Equity in Home | |
	Couples	Unrelated Individuals	Couples[c]	Unrelated Individuals[c]
None	26	42	*[d]	*[d]
$1–999	17	19		
$1000–2999	15	11	13	18
$3000–4999	8	6		
$5000–9999	12	9	24	26
$10,000–19,999	11	7	40	39
$20,000 or More	13	5	23	17
Total Percent	100[e]	100	100	100

Source: Based on data in Janet Murray, "Homeownership and Financial Assets: Findings from the 1968 Survey of the Aged," *Social Security Bulletin* 35 (August 1972):3–23.
[a]Age 65 or older.
[b]Asset information does not include value of business and farm assets and equity in rental.
[c]Homeowners only.
[d]Not applicable.
[e]Totals may not add up to 100 due to rounding.

atively insignificant amounts of *financial* assets. About two-thirds of elderly couples and almost 80 percent of unrelated individuals had less than $5000 in financial assets in 1967. In fact, 43 percent and 61 percent respectively had less than $1000.

Measuring Aged Poverty

The most popular measure of poverty in America today is the Social Security Administration's poverty index. Developed in the early 1960's, it gained prominence in the Johnson Administration's declared "War on Poverty." The index continues to be widely used today, despite the fact that the Nixon Administration—very early in its first term— discouraged government agencies from using the index, arguing that because of conceptual and measurement problems it was a misleading and unreliable measure.

A succinct description of the Social Security Administration's poverty index was presented in 1967 testimony by then Secretary of Health, Education, and Welfare Wilbur Cohen before the U.S. House Committee on Ways and Means (1967):

> The starting point for the SSA poverty index is the amount of money needed to purchase the food for a minimum adequate diet as determined by the Department of Agriculture. The food budget is the lowest that could be devised to supply all essential nutrients using food readily purchasable in the U.S. market (with customary regional variations). The poverty line is then calculated at three times the food budget (slightly smaller proportions for one- and two-person families) on the assumption—derived from studies of consumers—that a family that has spent a larger proportion of its income on food will be living at a very inadequate level. The food budgets and the derivative poverty income cutoff points are estimated in detail for families of differing size and composition (62 separate family types) with a farm/nonfarm differential for each type. This variation of the poverty measure in relation to family size and age of members is its most important distinguishing characteristic.
> Because the level of living implied by the poverty index is lower than we think most people would regard as an appropriate measure of adequacy of income for retired persons or disabled workers and their families or widows and children, we have also developed a slightly higher index. We call this the low-income index, and it is definitely low income.

It is an interesting fact that in actual practice the low-income index has rarely been used for policy evaluation purposes. Instead the poverty index has almost exclusively dominated the discussions of how many nonaged and aged are in economic difficulty and what policies are needed to deal with these difficulties. It is important, therefore, to understand how the poverty index is calculated and its limitations.

Calculating the Poverty Index   Because of its wide use and importance, let us run through step by step the construction of this poverty measure. First, as was indicated in Cohen's statement above, an amount of adequate food for the family unit is determined, and then the cost of that food at prevailing prices is ascertained by pricing foods in retail stores.

For about thirty years the Department of Agriculture has produced "food plans" that meet the nutritional standards set out by an organization called the National Research Council. While these plans meet nutritional standards, they also try to make the quantities and types of food chosen compatible with the general preferences of American families, preferences determined by food-consumption studies. It is not simply a matter of giving poor people only beans. General eating habits are taken into account.

Thus, in constructing a food plan an attempt is made to respond to the fact that people prefer meat to beans, although in terms of protein you can get more or at least as much protein from beans as you can from meat. The fact remains, however, that most of the protein in such plans is provided by nonmeat products.

It is also important to note that this food plan was originally devised for emergency periods only and that no one is expected to have to live over a long period of time on these very minimal food amounts. This implies that these food diets would be detrimental to your health over an extended period.

Finally, the Department of Agriculture makes no pretense in assuming that all families can skillfully budget or are willing to eat the foods specified in the plans. These assumptions need not be made, given the purpose of the plans. They were developed simply as a device to provide social welfare agencies with a needs standard that was not completely subjective in determining how much money poor people need to avoid serious malnutrition.

The next step in developing the poverty measure is to construct food budgets for different types of families. The poverty index is based on family units with different combinations of the following characteristics:

a. Age of head over or under age 65.
b. Size of family (2 to 7 or more).

    c. Farm and nonfarm.
    d. Male and female head of household.
    e. Number of related children under age 18.
    f. "Unrelated" family units.

The final step is to multiply the cost of the various food plans by three. As explained by the Social Security Administration:

> The Agriculture Department evaluated family food consumption and dietary adequacy in a 1955 survey week and reported for all families of two or more—farm and nonfarm—an expenditure for food approximating one-third of money income after taxes. Two-person nonfarm families used about 27 percent of their income for food and families with three or more persons about 35 percent. A later study made in 1960-61 by the Bureau of Labor Statistics found for urban families that nearly a fourth of a family's income (after taxes) went for food. There is less variation by size of family than might have been anticipated, ranging between 22 percent and 28 percent.... The earlier relationship based upon the Department of Agriculture's study was adopted as the basis for defining poverty—that is, an income less than three times the cost of the economy food plan for families of three or more persons. (U.S. House Committee on Ways and Means, 1967)

Thus we see that the "three" used to calculate the poverty level is based upon a survey of the ratio of food consumption to other expenditures of *all* families in the United States. Averaging all families, the Agriculture Department came out with an estimate of three. The Bureau of Labor Statistics' estimate of "four" was ignored by the Social Security Administration for unstated reasons.

Based on the resulting index, Table 10 shows 1973 poverty rates for various elderly families by work status and sex. The overall proportion of elderly with income below the poverty index has been falling—from 28 percent in 1966 to 16 percent in 1974.

The Retired Couples' Budget The second major way of measuring poverty is the Bureau of Labor Statistics' Retired Couples' Budget: "The retired couple is defined as a husband age 65 or over and his wife. They are self-supporting, living independently in their own home, in reasonably good health, able to take care of themselves."

Actually there are three budgets—indicative of three different levels of living. The illustrative family is assumed to have, for each budget level, *average inventories* of clothing, house furnishings, major durables, and other equipment. The budgets pertain only to *urban* families with the specified characteristics. No budgets are available for

Table 10   Poverty Rates[a]Among Aged[b] Families and Unrelated Individuals, by Work Status and Sex, 1973

| | *Percent Poor* | | | |
| | *Not Retired[c]* | | *Retired[d]* | |
Family Status	*Men*	*Women*	*Men*	*Women*
All 65 and Over	4.9	10.9	15.5	33.6
Family Head	4.2	*[e]	11.5	17.9
Unrelated Individual	9.8	11.4	31.9	37.3

Source: Unpublished data provided by the Social Security Administration, derived from special Office of Economic Opportunity tabulations.
[a]Percent poor.
[b]Age 65 or older.
[c]Worked year-round, full time; data for part-year or part-time workers not shown.
[d]Head or unrelated individual did not work during the whole year.
[e]Percentage not computed for base less than 50,000.

rural families. The budgets are not intended to represent a minimum or subsistence level of living but rather a level described by the Bureau of Labor Statistics as "modest but adequate."

The history of this budget is interesting. Originally the Bureau of Labor Statistics had only one budget for a *nonaged* family of four persons, first developed in 1946–47. It was recognized quite early, however, that it was inappropriate to measure what an older couple needed by referring to the expenditure needs of a family of four. This family, for example, has extra expenses for the clothing and education of the children.

Reacting to the different living situations of different families, the Social Security Administration developed concurrently with the Bureau of Labor Statistics' budget effort a separate budget for retired couples. In 1959 the Bureau of Labor Statistics revised the older couples' budget. This budget was then updated every three or four years to take account of price changes. But more importantly, the budget was periodically adjusted in an attempt to take into account general increases in the standard of living. Thus, for example, in the 1959 budget *five out of six* aged families were assumed to have home telephones (which were used for local calls only). By 1966 the budgets assumed that *all* older couples needed to have phones and that provision for some long-distance calls was appropriate.

One might wonder how the budget changes in living standards are determined. Most are based on "consumer expenditure surveys" of families with different incomes. As average income increases, average expenditures for different goods change. As described by the Bureau of

Labor Statistics, the amount chosen for the budget is "the point on the income scale where families stop buying 'more and more' and start buying either 'better and better' or something else less essential to them."

Using this technique means that a major part of the increase in changes in the budget level is due to changes in the real standard of living of individuals (rather than just price changes). So, the Bureau of Labor Statistics' budget standard is not locked into a mechanism similar to the Social Security Administration's three-times-the-food budget assumption.

Once again, however, the assumptions made are somewhat arbitrary. In the words of the Bureau of Labor Statistics, "In general, the representative list of goods and services comprising the standard of budget reflects the collective judgment of families as to what is necessary and desirable to meet the conventional and social as well as the physical needs of families in the present decade."

In the autumn of 1971 the Bureau of Labor Statistics issued for the first time not one but three budget levels for an aged couple: a "lower," an "intermediate," and a "higher" budget. The development of alternative budgets was in part stimulated by the fact that some people were saying the Bureau of Labor Statistics' budget was too high for their purposes, while others were saying it was too low:

> It has been evident that no single budget at one specified level would meet all of the important needs. Throughout the decade of the 1940's, for example, state public assistance agencies appealed to BLS [Bureau of Labor Statistics] to develop a budget for a lower living standard or to suggest ways in which the moderate budget could be scaled down. . . . On the other hand, representatives of voluntary social and welfare agencies providing services to families with a special problem. . .frequently requested budget estimates for a standard higher than moderate to consider in determining eligibility or establishing a scale of fees paid for the services provided. . .(U.S. Bureau of Labor Statistics, 1967).

The last major revision in the Retired Couple's Budget was in 1969. Since then the budget has been updated annually by adjusting costs for relevant changes in components of the Consumer Price Index. For the fall of 1974 the Bureau of Labor Statistics set the Retired Couple's Budget at $4228 (lower level), $6041 (intermediate level), and $8969 (higher level). (Rogers, 1975) Unfortunately, one result of the new multiple budgets is that we are now left with even more arbitrariness in interpretation; we do not have one budget but three to choose from—with no very explicit explanation as to why one should be used over the other. At least with the Social Security poverty index one can reason that the lower index is for emergency or temporary use and that the higher one indicates the amount necessary to permit a family to live and remain healthy over a longer period of time. On this basis one can argue that the lower Social Security index is not very good for policy purposes (i.e., long-run policy purposes) and therefore that we should use the higher one for most purposes.

Unfortunately, the whole general question of how best to measure poverty has received relatively little attention over the years. The poverty index originally developed by the Social Security Administration in the early 1960's has not undergone any revision since that time. It has merely been adjusted upward annually for changes in the Consumer Price Index.

The Education Act Amendments of 1974, however, specified that a federal intragovernmental agency committee review alternative ways of measuring poverty. It is hoped that the recommendations of this committee will serve as the basis for a broad review of the problem in the next few years. In the meantime, we must continue to rely on the existing measures with their various limitations.

The Impact of Inflation

Economic instability, causing unemployment and inflation, creates insecurity for families and individuals of all ages because of the uncertainty of when and how it will strike. For those actually affected, inflation or unemployment can have a major impact on their economic situation by changing the real value of their wealth or affecting their earning power.

The phenomenon of inflation is without doubt one of the least understood of economic occurrences.* Almost everyone feels *harmed* by inflation; yet the truth is that some people and institutions *gain* from inflation. One person's loss is typically somebody else's gain. The result is a redistribution of wealth and income that can be both quite drastic and quite haphazard.

While inflation affects people of all ages, we will restrict the discussion that follows to the older population. There are five principal ways older people can be affected adversely by *unanticipated* inflation:

*We can go only briefly into the economics of inflation in this book. Readers interested in a relatively nontechnical but more extensive discussion of the issue should read Solow (1975).

a. If net creditors, assets which do not adjust in value for inflation will depreciate in value, reducing the net worth of the individual or family.
b. If recipients of transfer (pensions, unemployment benefits, etc.) or other income, adjustments in these various income sources may lag behind inflation, reducing real income.
c. If employed, adjustments in earnings levels may lag behind inflation, reducing real wages.
d. If taxpayers, the real burden of federal and state income taxes may increase because the tax brackets in the laws are defined in *money* rather than *real* terms.
e. If inflation is concentrated among items such as food, which comprise a larger proportion of elderly persons' budgets, the older age group may be differentially affected—especially if indexes used to measure and adjust various sources of income do not correctly reflect aged buying patterns.

Wealth   It is with regard to the first item, the impact of inflation on the wealth position of the elderly, that the evidence is most clear. As we indicated earlier in this chapter, substantial *financial* assets are held by the elderly, but these assets are highly concentrated in the possession of a relatively small number of the aged. On the other hand, tangible assets—such as homes, automobiles, and the like—are held by a large proportion of the aged population.

In general the money value of tangible assets tends to increase with inflation, leaving the real value of this portion of the aged's wealth unaffected. But, apart from common stock and mutual funds, most *financial* assets do not adjust when the general level of prices changes. Persons holding bonds, checking accounts, savings accounts, and insurance policies find the real value of these assets falling with inflation; alternatively, persons with debts—such as an outstanding mortgage on a home—find the real value of these debts also falling (which is to their advantage).

A number of studies have investigated the effect of unanticipated inflation on the distribution of wealth among households. One of the findings from these studies is that when households are grouped according to age of head, *the largest decline in wealth occurs among families headed by elderly persons*. Alternatively, the largest *increase* in wealth occurs among the group age 25 to 34. It is the minority of the aged with substantial nonadjusting financial assets who are most severely affected. That is, for those aged fortunate enough to have substantial savings, inflation is often a serious problem.

Transfer Income   With regard to the second item, lagging transfer income, again the impact is relatively clear but in a way that will surprise some readers. Since persons living primarily on relatively "fixed incomes" are clearly hurt by rising prices and since the aged are so heavily dependent on pensions, the aged traditionally have been cited as "the" major group harmed by inflation.

While this was a major problem for the aged in years past, recent developments have substantially moderated it. *The major source of retirement income, the social security program, now adjusts benefits automatically for inflation.* Also, both the Supplemental Security Income (SSI) and food stamp programs for the poor aged automatically adjust their basic benefits for inflation. The three major income sources that do *not* adjust automatically are veterans' pensions, private pension benefits, and most supplemental state payments under SSI.* Also, the levels of allowable income determining eligibility for SSI, food stamps, and some Medicaid programs are not changed automatically.

Thus the bulk of aged transfer income currently adjusts automatically for inflation with a relatively short lag.

Earnings and Tax Brackets   Both of these items share the common characteristic of being very difficult to predict with regard to inflationary impact. While earnings generally increase over time, partly in response to inflation, earnings in particular firms or industries may lag behind inflation. Some of the aged still working will find this to be a problem, but in general few are affected because of the small number of the elderly who continue to work full time and because not all that do are employed in firms where earnings lag behind inflation.

Similarly, many aged do not pay income taxes because their incomes are low and social security income is tax exempt. Those who do, however, face two problems: some of the added income to compensate for inflation will be taxed away and, moreover, will be taxed away under progressive tax structures at progressively larger marginal rates.

Expenditure Patterns and Cost-of-Living Indexes   During inflationary periods, the prices of various goods change by different amounts. Since the expenditure patterns of individuals and families differ, any particular pattern of inflationary price increases will have a varying impact, depending on the particular expenditure patterns of various individuals. For example, if food and housing prices go up faster than other goods and services and if the aged spend a larger share of their income on food and housing, the result is a larger increase in prices paid by the aged than the nonaged.

*We discuss in Chapter 7 the problem of inflation depreciating private pension benefits.

Thus, it is often asserted that the Bureau of Labor Statistics Consumer Price Index (CPI), which is used to adjust social security benefits, is not a very good index for this purpose. It is argued that the CPI, which is constructed for a middle-income urban worker with a wife and two children, poorly represents the buying patterns of the elderly.

Several studies have investigated the need for a separate index for the elderly. Hollister and Palmer (1972) looked at the period 1947 to 1967; Theodore Torda (1972) reviewed the 1960–61 to mid-1972 period; and Thad Mirer (1974) studied the August 1971 to June 1974 period. The results of all three of these studies indicate that for the periods investigated, *the cost of living had not risen faster for the elderly than for other groups* and, thus, that the CPI did a good job of measuring inflation relative to the expenditure patterns of the elderly.

Suggested Readings

Aaron, Henry J. "What Do Circuit-breaker Laws Accomplish?" In George E. Peterson, ed., *Property Tax Reform*. Washington, D.C.: The Urban Institute, 1973.
  A provocative discussion of property-tax relief for the elderly that challenges the traditional assumption that homeowners "pay" the property tax and seriously questions the equity of such a tax. Readers interested in a more comprehensive and technical discussion should see Aaron's *Who Pays the Property Tax?* (Washington, D.C.: The Brookings Institution, 1975).

Bixby, Lenore E.; W. W. Finegar; S. Grad; W. W. Kolodrubetz; P. Lauriat; and J. Murray. *Demographic and Economic Characteristics of the Aged*. Office of Research and Statistics, Research Report No. 45. Washington, D.C.: U.S. Government Printing Office, 1975.
  The "1968 Survey of the Aged." This survey was a follow-up to the 1963 Survey of the Aged (see Epstein and Murray below). Like its predecessor, it provides the most comprehensive data available on the aged population in 1967.

Epstein, Lenore A., and Janet H. Murray. *The Aged Population of the United States*. Office of Research and Statistics, Research Report No. 19. Washington, D.C.: U.S. Government Printing Office, 1967.
  The "1963 Survey of the Aged." This was the first comprehensive survey of the United States aged in 1962. It includes information not gathered in the census or other sample surveys and analysis of this data by the staff of the Social Security Administration.

Mueller, Marjorie Smith, and Robert M. Gibson. "Age Difference in Health Care Spending, Fiscal Year 1974." *Social Security Bulletin* (June 1975): 3–16.
  An analysis of health expenditures, including sources of funds, types of expenditures, and trends since 1966.

Orshansky, Mollie. "Federal Welfare Reform and the Economic Status of the Aged Poor." In M. H. Morrison, et al., *The Supplemental Security Income Program for the Aged Blind and Disabled.* Office of Research and Statistics Staff Paper No. 17. Washington, D.C.: U.S. Government Printing Office, 1974, pp. 24–34.
> A discussion of the poor aged and the possible effects of the Supplemental Security Income program on them. Special attention is given to the problems of women.

Pen, Jan. *Income Distribution.* New York: Praeger, 1971.
> A very readable and comprehensive discussion of income distribution for readers interested in the general problems of measurement and research findings on the determinants of the distribution.

Social Security Bulletin. Washington, D.C.: U.S. Government Printing Office: monthly.
> This journal reports changes in social security and other similar legislation and also publishes the results of research studies by the Social Security Administration (and SSA sponsored research projects), various survey findings, and international social security developments.

Steiner, P.O., and R. Dorfman. *The Economic Status of the Aged.* Berkeley: University of California Press, 1957.
> A good historical view of the topic.

Taussig, Michael K. *Alternative Measures of the Distribution of Economic Welfare.* Princeton, N.J.: Industrial Relations Section, Princeton University, 1973.
> A study that develops measures of economic welfare that go beyond just money income.

U.S. House Select Committee on Aging. *Federal Responsibility to the Elderly.* Washington, D.C.: U.S. Government Printing Office, 1976.
> A set of charts compiled by the Congressional Research Service listing the major federal programs benefiting the elderly in the areas of: employment, health care, housing, income maintenance, social services, training and research, and transportation.

U.S. Senate Special Committee on Aging. *Developments in Aging.* Washington, D.C.: U.S. Government Printing Office: annually.
> This yearly report by the committee reviews a wide range of developments in aging, including economic aspects. An appendix contains reports from federal departments and agencies with specific activities affecting the elderly.

U.S. Senate Special Committee on Aging. *Economics of Aging: Toward a Full Share in Abundance.* Hearings: Parts 1-11 and various working papers. Washington, D.C.: U.S. Government Printing Office, 1969–1970.
> A collection of reports, working papers, and hearings covering a wide range of topics.

Appendix
A Socioeconomic Profile of the Aged*

Population Characteristics

Average Life Expectancy (at Birth)
               (Number of Years)

	1900	*1930*	*1973*	*2000*
White Men	46.6	59.7	68.4 }	69.6
Nonwhite Men	32.5	47.3	61.9 }	
White Women	48.7	63.5	76.1 }	75.8
Nonwhite Women	33.5	49.2	70.1 }	

Average Life Expectancy (at Age 60)
               (Number of Years)

	1900-02	*1929-31*	*1949-51*	*1973*
White Men	14.35	14.72	15.76	16.2
Nonwhite Men	NA (Not Available)	NA	NA	15.6
White Women	15.23	16.05	18.64	21.1
Nonwhite Women	NA	NA	NA	19.3

Average Life Expectancy at Various Ages, 1973
               (Number of Years)

	40	*50*	*65*	*70*
White Men	32.2	23.6	13.2	10.4
Nonwhite Men	28.7	21.5	13.1	10.7
White Women	38.5	29.5	17.3	13.7
Nonwhite Women	34.4	26.4	16.2	13.2

*For simplicity and ease of reading, the tables appearing in this section do not contain explanatory and qualifying information appearing as footnoes in the original sources. Hence readers should be cautious about using or reproducing the information without consulting the original sources.

Changing Population Age 45 and Older
(in Millions)

	1900	1930	1950	1974	2000
Age 45–54	6.4	13.1	17.4	23.8	35.7
Age 55–64	4.0	8.5	13.4	19.5	22.9
Age 65 and Over	3.1	6.7	12.3	21.8	30.6

Ratio of Women to Men in Various Age Groups
(Number of Women per 100 Men)

	1910	1930	1950	1974	2000
Age 45–54	} 87.1	} 91.6	100.3 }	} 109.2	103.5
Age 55–64			99.5		113.9
Age 65–74	} 99.8	} 99.4	107.6 }	} 143.3	133.9
Age 75 and Over			121.1		176.6

Blacks as a Proportion of the Aged Population, 1900–1974
(Percent)

	1900	1930	1950	1974
All Ages	11.6	9.7	9.9	11.4
Age 60 and Over	8.7	5.9	6.8	8.2
Age 65 and Over	8.5	5.6	7.0	7.9

Ethnic Composition of the Population Age 65 and Over
(Percent)

	1970 (Census)	1974 (Estimate)	1975 (Projected)
White	91.5	91.1	91.0
Negro	7.7	7.9	8.1
Spanish Origin	2.0	1.7	1.8
American Indian	0.8		
Japanese	0.2		
Chinese	0.2		
Filipino	0.1	} 0.9	} 0.9
Korean	0.01		
Hawaiian	0.02		
All Other	0.05		
Total	100.0	100.0	100.0

States with the Largest Proportion of Persons Age 65 and Over, 1974

Rank	State	Persons Age 65 and Over	Percent of State Population
1	Florida	1,267,000	15.7
2	Arkansas	264,000	12.8
3	Iowa	360,000	12.6
4	Kansas	281,000	12.4
4	Missouri	591,000	12.4
4	Nebraska	191,000	12.4
7	South Dakota	84,000	12.3
8	Oklahoma	328,000	12.1
9	Rhode Island	111,000	11.8
10	Maine	122,000	11.7

States with the Largest Aged Populations, 1970

Rank	State	Persons Age 65 and Over	Percent of State Population
1	New York	1,961,000	10.8
2	California	1,801,000	9.0
3	Pennsylvania	1,272,000	10.8
4	Illinois	1,094,000	9.8
5	Ohio	998,000	9.4
6	Texas	992,000	8.9
7	Florida	989,000	14.6
8	Michigan	753,000	8.5
9	New Jersey	697,000	9.7
10	Massachusetts	636,000	11.2

States with the Largest Aged Populations, 1974

Rank	State	Persons Age 65 and Over	Percent of State Population
1	New York	1,998,000	11.0
2	California	1,986,000	9.5
3	Pennsylvania	1,348,000	11.4
4	Florida	1,267,000	15.7
5	Illinois	1,134,000	10.2
6	Texas	1,120,000	9.3
7	Ohio	1,050,000	9.8
8	Michigan	798,000	8.8
9	New Jersey	749,000	10.2
10	Massachusetts	661,000	11.4

Social Characteristics

Marital Status of Persons Age 55 and Over, 1974
(Percent)

	Persons Age 55–64	Persons Age 65–74	Persons Age 75 and Over
Men			
Single	6.1	4.3	5.0
Married	85.8	84.3	68.0
Widowed	4.1	8.9	25.2
Divorced	4.0	2.4	1.8
	100.0	100.0	100.0
Women			
Single	5.5	6.6	6.0
Married	69.3	47.6	24.4
Widowed	20.5	42.6	68.1
Divorced	4.7	3.2	1.5
	100.0	100.0	100.0

Marital Status of Persons Age 65 and Over
(Percent)

	1965	1970	1975
Men			
Single	6.6	7.8	4.6
Married	71.3	71.8	78.9
Widowed	19.5	18.1	14.4
Divorced	2.6	2.4	2.2
	100.0	100.0	100.0
Women			
Single	7.7	7.7	6.3
Married	36.0	35.5	38.7
Widowed	54.4	54.6	52.4
Divorced	1.9	2.3	2.6
	100.0	100.0	100.0

Living Arrangements of Persons Age 65 and Over Living Outside of Institutions

(Percent)

	1970	1975
In Households	99.2	99.8
Head of Household	64.1	67.5
Wife or Other Relative of Head	33.2	31.2
Lodger or Resident Employee	2.0	1.1
In Non-Institutional Group Quarters	.8	.2

Changing Educational Background of Persons Age 55 and Over
(Median Years School Completed)

	1940		1950		1974
Age	Men	Women	Men	Women	Men and Women
55–59	8.2	8.4	8.4	8.6	
60–64	8.2	8.3	8.3	8.4	
65–69	8.1	8.2	8.1	8.3	10.3
70–74	8.0	8.2	8.0	8.3	
75 and Over	7.7	8.1	7.9	8.2	

Changing Educational Background of Persons Age 25 and Over
(Median Years School Completed)

	1940	1950	1974
Men	8.6	9.0	12.4
Women	8.7	9.6	12.3

Changing Educational Background of Nonwhite Persons Age 25 and Over
(Median Years School Completed)

	1940	1950	1974
Male	5.4	6.4	10.5
Female	6.1	7.2	10.9

Labor Force Characteristics

Occupational Distribution of Employed Workers Age 45 and Over
(Percentage)

	1950		1960		1970	
	Men	Women	Men	Women	Men	Women
Professional and Technical	6.7	13.6	8.3	13.9	11.6	14.5
Farmers and Farm Managers	14.3	1.6	8.5	1.0	4.6	0.4
Managers, Officials, Proprietors	14.1	7.1	13.8	5.6	13.8	5.4
Clerical	5.5	17.3	6.1	22.2	7.1	28.8
Sales Workers	5.6	8.9	6.4	9.2	7.2	8.8
Craftsmen and Foremen	19.5	1.8	20.4	.2	22.2	2.1
Operatives	15.2	18.1	17.0	15.2	17.6	15.5
Private Household	.3	11.7	0.2	1.0	0.1	6.0
Service	7.5	14.3	7.1	14.4	8.7	17.1
Farm Laborers	2.9	2.9	2.1	1.1	1.6	0.5
Laborers, except Farm	7.4	0.8	6.1	.5	5.4	0.9
Total	100.0	100.0	100.0	100.0	100.0	100.0

Labor-Force Participation Rates
(Percent)

	1890	1920	1950	1970	1990
Men Age:					
45–54	92 }	91 }	88	93	92
55–64	68 }	56 }	41	82	78
65 and over				26	19
Women Age:					
45–54	12 }	17 }	29	54	58
55–64	8 }	7 }	8	43	46
65 and over				9	8

Full-Time Versus Part-Time Work by Nonagricultural
Workers Age 65 and Over

(Percent)

	1957	1967	1970	1973
Men Working:				
Full Time	80	66	63	59
Voluntary Part Time	20	34	37	41
	100	100	100	100
Women Working:				
Full Time	62	54	53	50
Voluntary Part Time	38	46	47	50
	100	100	100	100

Work Experience of Women Age 55 and Over, 1974

Work Experience	Age 55–59	Age 60–64 (Percent)	Age 65 and Over
Worked in 1974	54.0	42.8	12.8
Did Not Work in 1974	46.0	57.2	87.2
Worked at Full-Time Jobs	75.4	71.2	39.3
50–52 Weeks	56.8	52.4	23.5
27–49 Weeks	12.1	10.6	6.3
1–26 Weeks	6.5	8.2	9.5
Worked at Part-Time Jobs	24.6	28.8	60.7
50–52 Weeks	12.7	11.9	28.4
27–49 Weeks	5.4	7.6	14.0
1–26 Weeks	6.4	9.3	18.3

Income Characteristics

Money Income Sources for Persons Age 65 and Over, 1967
(Percent)

Source	Total Age 65 and Over	Married Couples	Nonmarried Persons		
			Total	Men	Women
Earnings	27	46	15	19	14
Wages and Salaries	21	36	12	14	12
Self-Employment	6	12	3	5	2
Retirement Benefits	89	90	89	91	88
OASDHI	86	87	85	86	84
Other Public Pensions	10	11	9	11	8
Railroad Retirement	4	5	3	5	3
Government Employee	6	7	5	6	5
Private Group Pensions	12	19	7	13	5
Veterans' Benefits	10	12	9	11	8
Unemployment Insurance	1	2	1	1	1
Public Assistance	12	6	15	14	16
Income from Assets	50	60	44	44	45
Private Individual Annuities	2	2	2	1	2
Personal Contributions	3	2	4	2	5

Money Income Sources for Families with Head Age 65 and Over, 1974
(Percent)

Source	Percent of Families with Income from Designated Source
Earnings	
Wage or Salaries	43.2
Nonfarm Self-Employment	8.5
Farm Self-Employment	5.9
Social Security and Government Railroad Retirement	90.6
Dividends, Interest, Rents, Trusts, and Royalties	62.3
Public Assistance and Welfare Payments	9.9
Unemployment, Workmen's Compensation, Government Employee Pensions, and Veterans' Payments	22.0
Private Pensions, Annuities, Alimony, etc.	28.0

Median Income of Families with Head Age 65 and Over
(Dollars)

	1959	1970	1974
White	$3377	$5263	$6133
Black	$1755	$3281	$4354

Proportion of Persons Age 65 and Over with Money Incomes Below
Poverty Level
(Percent)

	1959	1967	1974
In Families	27	20	8.5
Head	29	21	9.5
Male	29	21	8.9
Female	29	26	13.0
Other Family Members	25	18	7.3
Not in Families	62	55	31.8
Male	59	45	26.8
Female	63	59	33.2
All White Aged	33	28	13.8
All Negro Aged	63	53	36.4

Expenditure Characteristics

Distribution of Consumer Expenditures by Age of Head for Urban U.S.
(Percent)

	1950		1960	
	Age 65–74	Age 75 and Over	Age 65–74	Age 75 and Over
Food and Alcoholic Beverages	33.0	33.5	31.2	31.4
Housing	19.2	22.7	20.4	24.1
Household Operation & Furnishings	10.5	11.7	10.1	11.7
Clothing	8.8	7.8	88.0	7.0
Transportation	11.9	9.4	12.7	9.9
Medical Care	7.0	6.9	7.8	7.7
Personal Care	2.1	1.8	2.2	1.9
Recreation	3.2	2.2	3.0	2.1
Other	4.3	41.0	4.7	4.3
Total	100.0	100.0	100.0	100.0

Proportion of Persons Age 55 and Over Who Own Homes
(Percent)

	1949	1960	1971
Family Head Age 55–64	62	62	74
65 and over	59	65	76

Proportion of Persons Age 55 and Over Who Own Automobiles
(Percent)

	1964	1967	1971
Family Head Age 55–64	78	76	83
65 and over	51	56	65

Sources

Population Characteristics

Life Insurance Fact Book 1975. New York: Institute of Life Insurance, undated.
U.S. Bureau of the Census. Census of Population: 1970. *General Population Characteristics.* Final Report PC(1) B-1. Washington, D.C.: U.S. Government Printing Office, 1970.
———. *Current Population Reports.* Series P-25, No. 529. "Estimates of the Population of the United States, by Age, Sex, and Race: July 1, 1974 and April 1, 1970." Washington, D.C.: U.S. Government Printing Office.
———. *Current Population Reports.* Series P-25, No. 493. "Projections of the Population of the United States by Age and Sex: 1972 to 2020." Washington, D.C.: U.S. Government Printing Office, 1972.
———. *Historical Statistics of the United States.* Washington, D.C.: U.S. Government Printing Office, 1961.
———. *Statistical Abstract of the United States: 1975.* Washington, D.C.: U.S. Government Printing Office, 1975.
U.S. Bureau of the Census, *Statistical Abstract of the United States: 1975* (Washington, D.C.: U.S. Government Printing Office, 1975).
U.S. Department of Health, Education and Welfare. *Facts About Older Americans 1975.* DHEW Pub. No. (OHD) 75-20006. Washington, D.C.: U.S. Government Printing Office, 1975.

Social Characteristics

U.S. Bureau of the Census. Census of Population: 1970. *General Population Characteristics.* Final Report C(1) B-1. Washington, D.C.: U.S. Government Printing Office, 1970.

———. *Current Population Reports.* Series P-20, No. 287. "Marital Status and Living Arrangements: March 1975." Washington, D.C.: U.S. Government Printing Office, 1975.
———. *Historical Statistics of the United States.* Washington, D.C.: U.S. Government Printing Office, 1961.
———. *Statistical Abstract of the United States, 1975.* Washington, D.C.: U.S. Government Printing Office, 1975.

Labor Force Characteristics

Beverly Johnson McEaddy. "Women in the Labor Force: The Later Years." *Monthly Labor Review* 98 (November 1975): 17–35.
Manpower Report of the President. Washington, D.C.: U.S. Government Printing Office, 1975.
U.S. Bureau of the Census, *Characteristics of the Population:* 1950, 1960, 1970. Washington, D.C.: U.S. Government Printing Office, 1950, 1960, 1970.
———. *Historical Statistics of the United States.* Washington, D.C.: U.S. Government Printing Office, 1961.
———. *Statistical Abstract of the United States: 1975.* Washington, D.C.: U.S. Government Printing Office, 1975.

Income Characteristics

Lenore E. Bixby, et al. *Demographic and Economic Characteristics of the Aged: 1968 Social Security Survey.* U.S. Social Security Administration/Office of Research and Statistics. Research Report No. 45/DHEW Publication No. (SSA) 75-11802. Washington, D.C.: Department of HEW, undated.
U.S. Bureau of the Census. *Current Population Reports.* Series P-60, No. 101, "Money Income in 1974 of Families and Persons in the United States." Washington, D.C.: U.S. Government Printing Office, 1976.
———. *Statistical Abstract of the United States, 1974.* Washington, D.C.: U.S. Government Printing Office, 1974.
———. *Statistical Abstract of the United States, 1975.* Washington, D.C.: U.S. Government Printing Office, 1975.

Expenditure Characteristics

Survey Research Center, Institute for Social Research, University of Michigan. *Survey of Consumer Finances.* Ann Arbor, Mich.: Braun-Brumfield, various years.
Sydney Goldstein. "Changing Income and Consumption Patterns of the Aged, 1950-1960." *Journal of Gerontology* 20, No. 4 (October 1965).

Chapter Three

To Work or
Not to Work

Every individual during his lifetime makes important choices regarding the type and amount of work to be undertaken. The individual chooses some combination of work in the labor force (paid and volunteer), unpaid work in the nonmarket sector, and leisure. Economists emphasize the trade-off between, on the one hand, work—which produces goods and services or results in income to buy the goods and services of others—and, on the other hand, leisure—which in itself is something that people also find useful or valuable. Thus, more leisure is bought at the expense of fewer goods and services for the whole economy.

The Work/Leisure Trade-off

Measuring work in terms of hours per week, we begin at a zero level in early childhood. At some point the individual might start a paper route, do some baby-sitting, or engage in some other part-time work. In the teenage years, part-time work may increase and some begin full-time work. Others go to college and "stop work." Through the middle years most men and about one-third of all women work in the labor force full time; most women also work in the nonmarket sector and some work part time in the labor force. When individuals reach age 65 (or, increasingly, earlier) work stops abruptly for many. This brief summary approximates the work pattern of the typical American worker today. Granted, of course, there are lots of variations to this pattern.

Professor Juanita Kreps (1971) has written about the number of hours individuals in various other countries spend in the paid labor force:

> The length of the workyear, determined by the number of hours worked per week and the number of weeks worked per year, must take

into account not only average weekly hours but the amount of time allowed for annual vacations and holidays . . . . For the full-time factory worker in the various countries, very rough estimates can be made of the number of hours worked per year . . . . The range between Sweden's short and Switzerland's long workyear is thus more than 400 hours, or about 10 weeks annually. Of the three intermediate countries, the United States stands about midway between the two extremes set by Sweden and Switzerland, while Germany and the United Kingdom have workyears which more nearly approach that of Switzerland.

Paid employment results in the economic output—gross national product—measured by national income–accounting techniques and reported regularly by government statistics. *Nonmarket work*, not included in the national income accounts, adds significantly to total output; Nordhaus and Tobin (1973) estimate that in 1965, for example, nonmarket work equaled 48 percent of gross national product. *Not working* translates into a given amount of leisure over the lifetime.

Let us suppose a country wants to hold constant the total amount of work and leisure over the lifespan but wishes to alter the way in which they are currently distributed. One of the things that can be done is to try to figure out at what point in the life cycle it might be appropriate to taper off weekly hours of work, if the option were available. Providing more leisure in this way (i.e., by reducing hours of work) means, however, that some people *must work more* some other time—later or earlier in their lives. Realistically, providing increased leisure without a significant drop in lifetime income probably means working longer when older.

Professors Kreps and Spengler (1966) give us some illustrations of the options we face. Figure 3 presents their projections of the various possibilities of additional gross national product (GNP) and/or leisure available over a twenty-year period (1965–1985). As the various factors influencing economic growth (technological change, investment, rising quality of labor, etc.) increase productivity, new opportunities for increased leisure arise.

With regard to the possible future growth in leisure and its probable distribution. . .at one extreme, assuming no change in working time, per capita gross national product could rise from $3181 in 1965 to $5802 in 1985, or by about 80 percent. At the other extreme, if one supposes that all growth is taken in leisure time except the amount necessary to keep per capita GNP constant at $3181, the possible changes in working time would be as follows: the workweek could fall to 22 hours, or the workyear could be limited to 27 weeks per year, or retirement age could be lowered to 38 years, or almost half the labor force could be kept in retraining programs, or additional time available for education might well exceed our capacity to absorb such education.

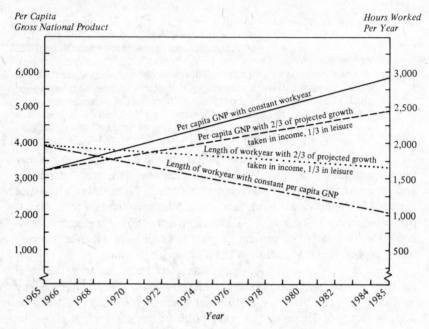

Per Capita
Gross National Product

Hours Worked
Per Year

Figure 3. Alternative Uses of Economic Growth Per Capita
Gross National Product and Hours Worked, 1965–85

Source: Juanita Kreps and Joseph Spengler, "The Leisure Compon-
ent of Economic Growth," in National Commission on Technology,
Automation and Economic Progress, *The Employment Impact of
Technological Change,* Appendix Vol. II (Washington, D.C.: U.S.
Government Printing Office, 1966), pp. 353–389.

If one takes all the increased growth potential in the form of
greater per capita output, Kreps and Spengler estimate that by the year
1985 we could almost double the level of per capita output over what it
was in 1965. This projection assumes that there are no "costs to
growth," an assumption increasingly questioned by economists. Some of
the growth, for example, will have to go into pollution control devices,
sewage treatment plants, and defense (tanks and bombs); to say that this
growth in output represents an increase in our standard of living is
stretching a point.

Also the projections assume that the government allows the potential growth to occur by use of appropriate monetary and fiscal policy*

*Monetary and fiscal policy refers to government action to influence the demand
for and supply of money (monetary policy) and direct changes in government expenditures
and/or tax levels (fiscal policy).

and that the assumptions with regard to future changes in technology and the growth of capital based upon "past" occurrences are correct.

Accepting these qualifications, Figure 3 attempts to show that one major option available to the nation is increasing the future real standard of living of individuals in the society by a sizable amount. Alternatively we can choose less goods and services but more leisure.

What are the reasons many professionals advocate changes in our present mix of work and leisure? Why do some urge, for example, that we stop the trend toward earlier retirement?

Many medical doctors are concerned about the rising trend toward "no-work"; they claim that some people die earlier, partly as a result of the change from being physically and mentally active to a more sedentary lifestyle. Some social gerontologists have argued that termination of work results in psychological problems connected with the loss of social role and adjustment to retirement realities. Economists worry about the problems of financially supporting a growing retired population with its accompanying rise in public and private pension costs.

Many gerontologists urge that we introduce more flexibility or options into the retirement process. Some are particularly eager to abolish institutionalized retirement. There is a real question, however, as to whether a society can ever introduce meaningful flexibility into the retirement process. So far nobody has figured out how to do it in a way that will have wide appeal to both employers and employees.

The fact is that during the past two decades, mandatory retirement—plus the social security retirement test and private pension vesting—has dominated older-worker employment policy discussions. While advocates on behalf of the aged have been almost unanimous in calling for an end to (or more flexibility in) mandatory retirement-age policies, there is no evidence of any decline in the existence of such provisions. In fact, some people fear there has been a trend toward less, not more, flexibility.

Studies have shown that the social security retirement test in the United States has a strong negative influence on the willingness of the elderly to continue working. The debate over this provision of the social security law has been intense.*

In contrast to practice in the United States, some countries encourage work beyond age 65. For example, workers in certain countries are not penalized by loss of or a reduction in social security benefits if they continue to work. Others, like the United States, impose retirement tests, which limit the amount of work persons can engage in (or earnings received) and still be eligible for all or part of their social security pension

*See Chapter 6 for additional discussion of the retirement test.

benefits. Table 11 shows that the number of noncommunist, industrial countries without a social security retirement test is quite large—about 50 percent. When you reach age 65 in Sweden and Germany, for example, you get your benefits whether you work or not. Recently Norway introduced a flexible retirement test that permits persons age 67 to 69 who wish to continue working on a less than full-time basis to claim a partial pension if the sum of pension and earnings does not exceed 80 percent of former earnings.

Table 11   Prevalence of Retirement Tests in Social Security Systems, 1973

	Work Limitations While Collecting Benefits		
	No Limitations on Work	Partial Limitations on Work[a]	No Work Allowed
Noncommunist Industrial Nations	10	8	2
Communist Nations	1	7	3
Developing Nations	11	9	36
Total	22	24	41

Source: Based on data in Elizabeth Kreitler Kirkpatrick, "The Retirement Test: An International Study," Social Security Bulletin (July 1974): 3–16.
[a]Some countries eliminate the test at a certain age, usually 65 or 70 for men (and often earlier for women).

The eligibility age for retirement benefits also has a very important influence on the average age of retirement in all countries. Most industrialized countries set the eligibility age for normal retirement at 65. Despite these common elgibility ages, Table 12 shows considerable variation among nations in the proportion of people working after age 65.

Figure 4 shows labor-force participation in the United States by age for men over 54 in 1950 and 1968. In recent years there has been a very sharp drop in participation during the later years. Withdrawals from the labor force cluster around the eligibility ages for initial and regular social security pension benefits.

In contrast, the proportion of females in the labor force has risen sharply in every age group with an overall increase from 26 percent in 1940 to 40 percent in 1970. Moreover, the labor-force participation rate of women age 65 or more rose from 6 percent in 1940 to 10 percent in 1970.

Table 12   Percent of Persons Age 65 and Over Who Are Economically Active

Australia	11.7
Austria	4.9
Belgium	6.3
Canada	17.2
Democratic Republic of Germany	2.3
Denmark	18.9
England/Wales	11.4
Federal Republic of Germany	11.7
Finland	7.5
France	17.1
Greece	26.5
Ireland	26.2
Italy	12.9
Japan	34.9
Netherlands	7.3
Northern Ireland	11.5
Norway	21.2
Portugal	29.5
Scotland	11.3
Spain	11.2
Sweden	8.6
Switzerland	18.9
United States	16.2
U.S.S.R.	16.9 males[a]
	5.8 females[a]
Yugoslavia	30.6

Sources: Richard H. Rowland, "Withdrawal from the Work Force among Persons of Retirement Age in the USSR: 1959–1970," *Industrial Gerontology* (Spring 1975); *United Nations Demographic Yearbook* (New York: United Nations), 1972, 1973; *1973 Year Book of Labour Statistics* (Geneva: International Labour Office, 1973); Paul Fisher, "Labor Force Participation of the Aged and The Social Security System in Nine Countries," *Industrial Gerontology* (Winter 1975).
[a]Age 60 and over.

Economic Problems of Older Workers

The remainder of this chapter looks at the economic problems confronting older workers. In recent years there has been increasing recognition of the fact that a variety of special economic problems confront middle-aged and older workers: (a) age discrimination in hiring, (b) job obsolescence, (c) changing job-performance capabilities, which cause the need for job change (or job redesign), and (d) adverse institutional structures (such as mandatory retirement). In addition, older workers, while often protected by seniority against job loss, generally find themselves

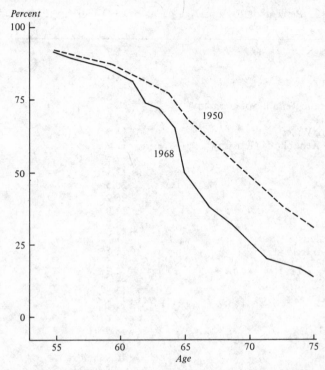

Figure 4. Changes in Labor-Force Participation, 1950 Versus 1968

Source: Howard N. Fullerton, "A Table of Expected Working Life for Men, 1968," *Monthly Labor Review* (June 1971).

almost as vulnerable as younger workers to plant shutdowns and many of the dislocations arising from mergers and government spending cutbacks. Not only do these problems often create immediate difficulties for workers and their families, but they also have an economic impact on their situation during the retirement years. Long-term unemployment, for example, makes saving difficult if not impossible. Moreover, periods of unemployment often result in lower pension benefits in retirement.

These special employment problems associated with aging are part of a larger set of factors influencing individuals in their decisions to work or not to work. In this regard, economists talk about labor-force participation and seek to understand the choices made in the relative amounts of time allocated between work and leisure, the latter including home work, volunteer work, and leisure. In contrast to the "retirement preparation" discussion in the next chapter, we will emphasize in this section the institutional pressures and constraints placed on individuals

Table 13   Unemployment Rates by Sex and Age, 1974
(Percent)

	16–17	18–19	20–24	25–34	35–44	45–54	55–64	Over 64
Men	18.5	13.3	8.7	3.9	2.6	2.4	2.6	3.3
Women	18.2	15.4	9.5	6.2	4.6	3.7	3.3	3.7

Source: *Manpower Report of the President* (Washington, D.C.: U.S. Government Printing Office, 1975), Table A-19.

in their determination of *when* to retire. We begin with a discussion of some of the economic problems confronting older workers and end with a discussion of "the retirement decision."

An important distinction in terminology must be kept in mind when reading the remainder of this chapter. Throughout most of the book when we talk about "the aged" or older persons, we are usually referring to those over age 65. In this chapter we talk about "older workers" but are not focusing exclusively or even primarily on persons over age 65. Rather, the major focus of this chapter is on workers who have reached middle age and those approaching retirement age (generally, the 45–65 age group).

Work Problems   As shown in Table 13, unemployment rates decline sharply with age but tend to be slightly higher in the later years than in the middle years. Insulated from unemployment by job-dismissal customs and formal seniority rules, older workers are not as likely to lose their jobs. With changing consumer expenditure patterns, however, many established industries have experienced a stagnation or gradual decline in employment opportunities. In contracting or closing businesses even senior jobholders are adversely affected. Declines, for example, in the cotton and woolen textile, agriculture, railroad, and shoe industries have encouraged or forced millions of workers to seek alternative jobs. Older workers confronted by a job change often find themselves faced with a variety of problems.

There has been a clear bias in private and public employment policy against older workers. Older workers have been discfiminated against in job hiring. Work and job structures have been made relatively inflexible, making mid-career adjustments very difficult. And various policies have encouraged or forced workers to retire and then have discouraged or prevented them from returning to the work force.

In 1965 the nation was made aware of the extent and nature of discrimination toward older workers through a report issued by the Department of Labor. This report documented that at that time more than 50 percent of all available job openings were closed to applicants over age 55 because of employers' policies *not* to hire any person over that age. Moreover, about 25 percent of the job openings were closed to applicants over age 45.

Since its passage in 1967, the federal Age Discrimination in Employment Act has attempted to protect individuals from age discrimination in matters of hiring, discharge, compensation, and other terms of employment. This law covers (with some exceptions) persons between the ages of 40 and 65. As a result, the more blatant signs of discrimination—such as newspaper ads restricting jobs to younger persons—have declined significantly.

It is difficult to determine, however, the extent to which actual discrimination has in fact lessened since little comprehensive evidence exists on the matter. Data on older-worker unemployment, however, are regarded by many as one important indicator that serious problems still exist. Studies show that while unemployment is relatively low among men age 45–65, those men in this age group who become unemployed typically remain unemployed much longer than younger workers.

The longer average duration of unemployment experienced by older workers is not all caused by age discrimination, however. Often older workers lack the necessary skills to qualify for available jobs or are not living in areas where job opportunities exist. Competing for jobs in the growing electronics and computer industries, for example, is difficult for many older workers. Many skills developed in the old established industries cannot be readily used in the "new technology" industries. And no large-scale programs exist in the United States to provide these older workers with the required newer skills.

Moreover, the problems arising from this incompatibility of skills have been aggravated by shifts in industries from their locations in the Northeast, Middle Atlantic, and North Central states to the Southeast, Southwest, and West. Many older workers with usable skills have been left behind with little hope for suitable new employment.

With the growth of private pensions has come the recognition that this fringe benefit in the pay package represents another possible factor contributing to the reemployment problems of older workers. Management may be reluctant to hire older workers because it is usually more costly to provide such workers with a specified pension benefit. This higher cost results primarily from two factors: (a) a shorter work history over which employer pension contributions must be made and thus lower investment income arising from the pension contributions, and (b) a declining probability with age of employee withdrawal (job turnover) between hiring and retirement. That is, the later the age of job entry, the shorter the period over which contributions can be made, the shorter the period over which interest is earned on the pension funds, and the less likely the worker will die or leave the plan before qualifying for any benefit. "Very definitely, then, most employers with pension plans have added costs if they hire older workers. If anything the differential has increased in the last decade, making it relatively even more costly to employ the experienced jobseeker."(Taggart, 1973)

Finally, evidence indicates that older workers have difficulty finding new jobs because of their "job-seeking" behavior and the lower priority given to them by various manpower agencies. Sobel and Wilcock (1963) in a study of 4000 job-seekers found that older workers displayed less willingness (a) to change types of work methods or methods of looking for work, (b) to engage in job retraining, (c) to adjust salary expectations, and (d) to move to areas of higher employment opportunity. Sheppard and Belitsky (1966) in a study of 500 workers in one locality found that older workers were also "more restrictive" in their job search techniques and less persistent in their activities.

Older workers often get lower-priority attention by government agencies set up to aid the unemployed. A 1973–74 study by the National Institute of Industrial Gerontology reaffirms earlier findings of the Sheppard and Belitsky study: there are no age differences in the proportion of unemployed persons seeking job assistance from the employment service but there is differential treatment by age. Figure 5 shows by age group the proportion of various employment service applicants receiving employment services, referral to a job, and placement in a job. Significantly fewer older workers were (a) tested, counseled, or enrolled in training, (b) referred to employers for job interviews, or (c) actually placed in a job. Likewise, while older workers constitute a large proportion of the long-term unemployed, they have always been an almost insignificant proportion of persons trained under the various manpower and training programs operated or financed by federal and state governments.

The Retirement Decision   In view of traditional work-oriented values in the United States and the importance of income derived from work, retirement is one of the most important decisions made by persons in our society. Aging in general and the retirement decision in particular, however, involve more complex and intertwined choices than deciding between more or less income. The amount of income and assets available is certainly one of the major considerations taken into account by most individuals in deciding when to retire. But there are other *personal considerations*. For example, the individual must consider his health and evaluate the physical and emotional difficulties of continued employment on a specific job vis-à-vis the benefits and problems of alternative employment or leaving the work force.

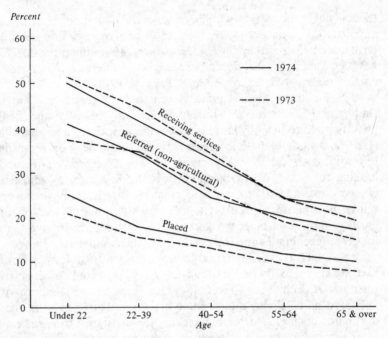

Figure 5.   Action Taken: Employment Service Applicants by Age

Source: Elizabeth M. Heidbreder and M. D. Batten, *ESARS II—A Comparative View of Services to Age Groups*, Facts and Trends No. 4 (Washington, D.C.: National Council on Aging, 1974).

Various *institutional realities* also affect the individual's retirement decision—factors which, in part, are beyond the person's own control. Included among these factors are such things as (a) the provisions of public and private pension plans, (b) changing pension levels and eligibility ages, (c) prospects for earnings levels, (d) job security and available employment opportunities, and (e) the institutional setting prescribed by work rules and government legislation.

Prior to 1962, men could not get social security benefits before age 65. In that year, the law was changed to allow men the same option granted to women in a 1956 amendment—early retirement at ages 62 through 64 with actuarially reduced benefits. The result was an immediate and major increase in the number of men opting for early retirement. Figure 6 shows the separation rates in 1970 for men age 55 to 73. It is clear that the social security eligibility age has a major impact on the willingness of workers to retire, despite the relatively low level of benefits paid.

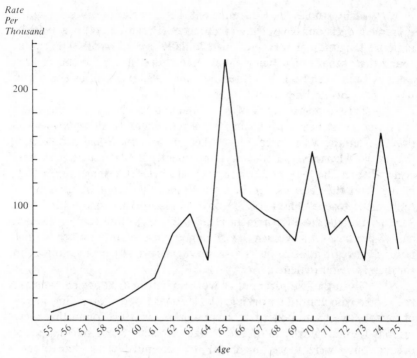

Figure 6. Male Retirement Separation Rates, 1970
Source: Unpublished data, U.S. Bureau of Labor Statistics.

Some workers apparently retire before age 65 because they can "afford to," often supplementing their reduced social security benefits with a private pension or other income. There is another group of workers who have already stopped working before the initial social security age of 62. The Social Security Administration's Survey of New Entitled Beneficiaries provides important new information on this group of workers. "Forty-one percent of the nonworking men entitled [becoming beneficiaries] at age 62 had been out of work for six months or more; 33 percent had not worked for at least a year; and 17 percent had been out of work three or more years."(Reno, 1971)

Deterioration of health is one of the most important factors encouraging early retirement. Some persons are unable to continue working because of disabling illness. Even those persons, who, despite health problems, could continue to work in their current, or perhaps in a less demanding job, may decide to retire at age 62—given the alternative income from a pension now available.

Many studies have documented the importance of health in the retirement decision. One of the most recent (Parnes, 1974) is a 1966–71 national longitudinal survey of men initially age 45 to 59. The survey found that, other things being equal, men with health problems in 1966 were twice as likely to have retired between 1966 and 1971 as those who were free of health limitations.

This survey study is of particular interest because it measured the influence of health problems *before* retirement on *subsequent* withdrawal from the work force. Most other studies have asked people *after* they retire why they retired, and consequently it has not been entirely clear whether the high proportion who cite health reasons are, in fact, giving what they consider to be a more socially acceptable reason for retirement. Joseph Quinn (1975), for example, reports that in the Social Security Longitudinal Retirement History Survey, 11 percent of the men and 18 percent of the women reporting good health and "no health limitations" gave (in another part of the survey) health as a prime motivation for their *early* retirement.

Given the high dropout of workers before or at age 65, who are the people who continue working? A National Council on Aging survey of persons age 65 and over who were working in 1974 found that these persons were employed in the full range of occupations, but that some occupations "were more amenable" to continued work than others. Table 14 contrasts the occupational distribution of those over age 65 with two younger age groups. As compared with younger ages, the data show

Table 14   Occupational Distribution of Various Age Groups of Workers in 1974

Occupation	Total	Age 18–54	Age 55–64	Age 65 and Over
Professional	19	20	13	10
Manager, Official, Proprietor	11	11	11	18
Clerical Worker	13	13	10	8
Sales Worker	6	6	5	10
Skilled Craftsman, Foreman	22	23	19	11
Operative, Unskilled Laborer	15	15	18	15
Service Worker	10	9	15	17
Farmer, Farm Manager, Laborer	3	2	6	8
Other	1	1	3	3

Source: Elizabeth L. Meier, "Over 65: Expectations and Realities of Work and Retirement," *Industrial Gerontology*, No 2 (Spring 1975): 95–109.
aFull-time and part-time employment.

that four occupational categories have higher proportions of over-65 workers: (a) managers and proprietors, (b) sales workers, (c) service workers, and (d) agricultural occupations. These are the areas where there is a large degree of self-employment and part-time job opportunities and where fewer jobs are affected by mandatory retirement rules.

Mandatory Versus Flexible Retirement Options

During the past few decades, mandatory retirement rules have been introduced by a large number of organizations in both the private and public sector. The most comprehensive study of the prevalence and nature of retirement age rules is a 1961 Cornell University sample survey (Slavick, 1966) of industrial firms in the United States with fifty or more employees. Perhaps the study's most important finding was that industrial establishments without pension or profit-sharing plans overwhelmingly have flexible retirement policies (over 95 percent of establishments without pension plans, about two-thirds of those with only profit-sharing plans). Among all establishments with formal pension plans, the majority (60 percent) had a flexible age policy with no upper age limit. The remainder (40 percent) had either (a) compulsory retirement at the "normal retirement age" or at an age later than the "normal retirement age," or (b) some combination of retirement-age flexibility and compulsion.

But this surprisingly high incidence of *flexible* retirement rules is strongly related to establishment size. For example, 68 percent of the establishments with fifty to ninety-nine employees had flexible rules as compared to only 30 percent of establishments with five hundred or more. In fact, of six independent variables investigated, the Cornell study found that only "size of [entire] company" and the "retirement benefit" showed any significant association with the existence of flexible retirement age policy.

If mandatory retirement is more prevalent in large firms than in smaller ones, what proportion of workers is subject to such rules? Since the extent of mandatory retirement was measured by the Cornell study in 1961, the prevalence of such practices has increased. A survey of all wage and salary workers 45–59 years of age in 1966 (U.S. Manpower Administration, 1970) found 46 percent who said they faced compulsory retirement in their present place of employment. Again, as in the earlier Cornell study, workers in firms without private pension plans were not likely to be subject to such rules.

Thus, about a half of wage and salary workers are subject to possible mandatory job termination as a result of reaching some age maximum. How many, however, are *actually terminated* as a result of such rules?

A partial answer to the question "how many?" is provided by data found in the Social Security Administration's Survey of New Beneficiaries. In an analysis of the questionnaires completed by *men* age 62–65 who were not working at the time of the survey, the Social Security Administration reports that 12 percent indicated that compulsory retirement was "the most important reason for leaving their last job." And among social security beneficiaries entitled at age 66 or older, it was found that only 10 percent of the nonworking men and women surveyed said they left their last jobs because of a "compulsory retirement age" (4 percent) or because they had "reached retirement age" (6 percent). These findings indicate that the overwhelming bulk of retired workers is not directly affected by mandatory retirement rules.

To understand more clearly why so few workers' jobs are actually terminated by mandatory retirement rules, it is useful to break down the retirement population into categories. First of all, many workers are not subject to mandatory retirement rules because they work for establishments without such provisions. And, of course, all self-employed persons are unaffected by such provisions.

Next, it is important to realize that many workers potentially subject to such rules leave establishments *before* reaching the age maximum. "Early retirement" has become a normal occurrence in recent years, while retirement at or after the normal retirement age has become less common. Furthermore, as Streib and Schneider (1971) have recently documented, "not *all* persons subject to retirement at a certain chronological age are reluctant to retire; some welcome the step." And, of those who do *not* want to retire, a certain proportion is encouraged by health or physical condition to "accept" mandatory retirement and does not try to reenter the work force. Finally, some proportion of those able and willing to work does, in fact, seek and is successful in finding new jobs on a part-time or full-time basis. Figure 7 illustrates these various alternatives.

The percentage estimates shown in Figure 7 are based on a survey of social security beneficiaries and exclude those not covered by social security (e.g., federal and certain state and local government workers). The data show that about two out of five males (aged 65 or less) *who reach a compulsory retirement age* are able and willing to work but are not working. As the figure shows, however, these workers represent less than 10 percent of the total cohort of retired males.

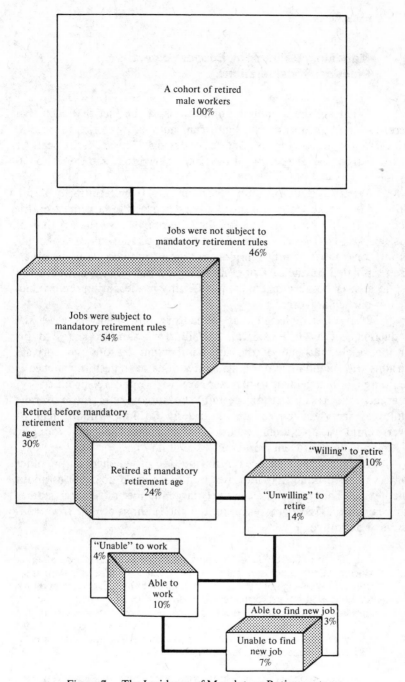

Figure 7. The Incidence of Mandatory Retirement

Source: James H. Schulz, "The Economics of Mandatory Retirement," *Industrial Gerontology*, Vol. 1, New Series (Winter 1974): 1–10.

Mandatory Retirement: Economic Versus Practical Considerations

What are the economic implications of the fact that each year there is a small proportion but significant number of workers forced to retire who would prefer to continue working? This question can be looked at from the perspective of the firm, the worker, and the nation as a whole.

Whether the firm gains economically from arbitrarily terminating older workers at some specified age depends in large part on the productivity and earnings level of those terminated versus (a) that of those workers hired as replacements (in the case of constant or expanding output), or (b) that of other employees of the firm who would be otherwise terminated (in the case of contracting output). The question is not easy to answer because of the great difficulty in measuring the productivity of particular workers.

It is often asserted that mandatory retirement increases the productivity of a business. Dan McGill, for example, states in his pension book that one of the most important reasons why private pensions with mandatory retirement provisions have been introduced is the desire of management to increase levels of work-force productivity. He argues that private pensions permit "the employer to remove overage employees from the payroll in an orderly fashion, without fear of adverse employee and public reaction, and to replace them with younger, presumably more efficient workers."(McGill, 1975)

A look at the evidence on the question of whether retiring older workers raises productivity indicates that one should be cautious about generalizing. The results of a relatively large number of research studies that bear on this issue are available, but the findings are far from conclusive or definitive:

> Collectively, leading studies on various aspects of the effects of aging document the conclusion that chronological age *alone* is a poor indication of working ability. Health, mental and physical capacities, work attitudes and job performance are *individual traits* at any age. Indeed, measures of traits in different age groups *usually* show *many* of the older workers to be superior to the average for the younger group and many of the younger inferior to the average for the older group. [Emphasis added.] (U.S. Dept. of Labor, 1965)

> Studies under actual working conditions show older workers performing as well as the younger if not better on most, but not all,

measures.... Age patterns of actual performance do not necessarily reflect the comparative capacities of all older persons versus younger people, but are traceable in part to labor market conditions and to selective processes that may, for example, retain in their jobs the competent older workers, promote the superior...or recruit [the] younger...of entirely different types.(Riley and Foner, 1968)

Factors working against older workers are (a) their on-average, *formal* education deficit compared to younger workers (which may or may not be offset by their greater on-the-job experience), (b) their being subject to a rising incidence of chronic illness and the possibility of declining physical and mental capacity, and (c) some degree of work assignment inflexibility due to the interaction of work rules, seniority systems, and pay scales. Although it is probably reasonable to assert that most employers recognize that the productivity of some of their older employees is as high or higher than that of younger workers, these employers also argue it is difficult (and costly) to identify such workers. Thus, they argue that mandatory retirement rules provide a practical administrative procedure that is objective, impersonal, and impartial and avoids charges of discrimination, favoritism, or bias in the termination process.

A 1974 national opinion survey conducted by Louis Harris and Associates for the National Council on the Aging collected interesting information on the "public's" reaction to this issue:

The public 18–64 and the public 65 and over were somewhat ambivalent about their attitudes toward mandatory retirement. Eighty-six percent (both groups) felt: "Nobody should be forced to retire because of age, if he wants to continue working and is still able to do a good job." About three-fifths agreed that "most people can continue to perform as well on the job as they did when they were younger." On the other hand, almost half (48 percent) of the 18–64 group, and more than half (54 percent) of those 65 and over agreed that "since many people are ready to retire at 65 years of age, and it's hard to make exceptions for those who are not ready, it makes sense to have a fixed retirement age for everyone."(Meier, 1975)

There has been an important initial effort to develop techniques for providing management with relatively objective ways of assessing workers' capabilities. In Canada, Dr. Leon Koyl has developed functional criteria to measure mental and physical fitness for various jobs. Koyl's system has been applied successfully for almost two decades by deHavilland Aircraft, Ltd. in Toronto, Canada. More recently, a demonstration project based upon the Koyl system was carried out in

Portland, Maine, by the National Council on the Aging. This project reported favorable results for the system as a job-placement instrument for workers over 40.(Batten, 1973)

Without operational measures of fitness, employers are faced with choosing among three options: (a) terminating workers arbitrarily, (b) allowing workers to decide when to retire, or (c) undertaking relatively expensive activities for "sorting out" the insufficiently productive older workers. More importantly, the employer must justify these termination decisions so that general worker morale will not be adversely affected. Historically, employers have been reluctant to opt for the first alternative (terminating workers solely on the basis of age)—especially given past levels of social security old-age pensions. But with the establishment of supplementary private pension plans, management (especially in larger firms) apparently feels such practices are much less inequitable.

In recent years the courts have upheld the rights of employers with mandatory retirement rules. In a Pennsylvania case the employee argued that the capability of individual employees to work beyond age 65 was not considered in the adoption of the mandatory retirement age and that no actuarial study to determine the effect of the action on the pension fund was undertaken. In February 1975, the Commonwealth Court of Pennsylvania ruled against the employee, holding that compulsory retirement at age 65 was an exception to prohibitions against age discrimination where employment is terminated because of the terms of a bona fide retirement plan (*Delvitto v. Shope, et al.*, No. 82 C.D. 1974, February 27, 1975).

And in the fall of 1975 the U.S. Supreme Court upheld the constitutionality of a Louisiana law requiring civil service employees to retire at age 65. Issuing no opinion of its own, the Court affirmed without comment the decision of a three-judge lower court. The lower court decision stated that there was a "rational basis" for mandatory retirement, since it was "fairly and substantially related" to a valid state objective of maintaining an "efficient, vigorous, and healthy civil service" and establishing a "feasible system for promotions of younger employees." (Pearl, 1976)

The mandatory retirement of employees willing and able to work results, of course, in a net loss of potention output to the nation as a whole to the extent that these workers are unable to find alternative employment. If we assume older workers are generally as productive as younger workers, a rough estimate of the annual loss is about $4 billion or about 0.3 percent of the total gross national product.

Policy Implications

At the same time that mandatory retirement rules have been increasing, significant changes have been occurring in the levels of social security and private pension benefits and the availability of early retirement options. These developments, along with a number of other factors, have resulted in a mammoth exodus of workers (potentially subject to maximum age rules) prior to the time when termination becomes mandatory.

With so many workers retiring before the age maximum and many of the remaining "voluntarily" retiring *at* the age maximum, why can't employers permit the relatively few who desire to do so to continue working? It would seem that the additional costs to the employer (if any) would be small, while the benefit to particular individuals is probably relatively high.

Many people are worried, however, that the trends are all in the opposite directions: that early and mandatory retirement will increase. If this is true, the historic decline in the role played by earnings from work to provide economic support in old age will continue. The importance of pension income in providing that support will continue to increase. And the costs of supporting people in retirement will also increase. In Chapters 5,6, and 7 we look at public and private pensions and the key role they play in the economics of aging. In Chapter 8 we discuss pension financing and the problem created by the declining retirement ages discussed in this chapter.

Suggested Readings

Blinder, Alan S. *Toward an Economic Theory of Income Distribution.* Cambridge, Mass.: The MIT Press, 1974.
    An advanced economic discussion of the work/leisure choice. Blinder develops a life-cycle model of consumption and bequest behavior and investigates the determinants of income distribution.
Boglietti, G. "Discrimination Against Older Workers and the Promotion of Equality of Opportunity." *International Labour Review* 110 (October 1974): 351–365.
    A review of older-worker problems in various countries throughout the world and a summary of the International Labour Office's action in this problem area.

Clague, Ewan; Balraj Palli; and Leo Kramer. *The Aging Worker and the Union—Employment and Retirement of Middle-Aged and Older Workers.* New York: Praeger, 1971.
One of the few books to give major attention to the unions' effect on older workers. It discusses, among other topics, antidiscrimination clauses in collective-bargaining agreements.

Kirkpatrick, Elizabeth Kreitler. "The Retirement Test: An International Study." *Social Security Bulletin* 37 (July 1973): 3–16.
Based on a survey of more than 100 countries, this article describes and discusses the wide variety of rules regarding the receipt of social security benefits when persons, otherwise eligible, work.

Kreps, Juanita. *Lifetime Allocation of Work and Income.* Durham, N.C.: Duke University Press, 1971.
A series of essays that discuss various aspects of work and leisure over the life-span.

Schulz, James H. "The Need for Age-Neutral Private Pensions." *Industrial Gerontology* 2 (Fall 1975): 255–263.
A discussion of the effect of private pensions on the employability of older workers.

Sheppard, Harold. "Work and Retirement." In Robert H. Binstock and Ethel Shanas, eds. *The Handbook of Aging and the Social Sciences.* New York: Van Nostrand Reinhold, 1976.
An up-to-date survey of the research in this area by one of the leading authorities in the industrial gerontology area.

U.S. Department of Labor. *The Older Worker.* Washington, D.C.: The U.S. Department of Labor, 1965.
Perhaps the most comprehensive government study of the discrimination and job problems of older workers.

U.S. Senate Special Committee on Aging. *Improving the Age Discrimination Law.* Washington, D.C.: U.S. Government Printing Office, 1973.
A history of the Age Discrimination in Employment law, discussion of its scope, information on Labor Department enforcement, and a review of various court decisions.

Chapter Four

Providing Retirement Income

We now shift from looking at employment problems and the retirement decision to issues connected with making financial provision for retirement. There are various ways in which individuals can provide income in the retirement years, those years when normal income received declines or from work/stops. Figure 8 lists the major mechanisms and institutions available in the United States today for providing economic assistance in retirement. These are divided into broad major groups —private versus public. The private mechanisms are either individual preparation or preparation undertaken by the individual as a part of group action. With the public mechanisms it is important to divided them by the criteria of whether or not there is a "means test" associated with the mechanism.

In this chapter the focus is primarily on private mechanisms, especially individual preparation for retirement. We are concerned with the job that faces an individual who wants to prepare for retirement. In the absence of group mechanisms, both public and private, what must the individual do to have adequate income in retirement?

We begin with this focus or emphasis not because this is the most common way that preparation for retirement is currently being carried out, nor because it is the most important way that we would expect it to be carried out in the future. Rather, beginning with individual preparation is a useful way of developing a good understanding of many of the concepts and issues involved in income-maintenance problems of old age. By starting at this level, it is easier to show some of the personal options, the major problems, and the magnitude of the retirement preparation task the individual faces. Thus, we can obtain some needed perspective on the whole problem.

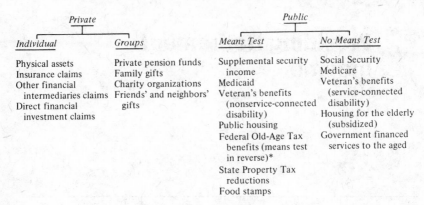

Private		Public	
Individual	*Groups*	*Means Test*	*No Means Test*
Physical assets	Private pension funds	Supplemental security	Social Security
Insurance claims	Family gifts	income	Medicare
Other financial	Charity organizations	Medicaid	Veteran's benefits
intermediaries claims	Friends' and neighbors'	Veteran's benefits	(service-connected
Direct financial	gifts	(nonservice-connected	disability)
investment claims		disability)	Housing for the elderly
		Public housing	(subsidized)
		Federal Old-Age Tax	Government financed
		benefits (means test	services to the aged
		in reverse)*	
		State Property Tax	
		reductions	
		Food stamps	

* Federal tax benefits can be utilized only by people with taxable income high enough to require that they pay taxes, hence take advantage of special tax provisions.

Figure 8.   Options for Retirement Income

Source: Adapted from James H. Schulz, Guy Carrin, Hans Krupp, Manfred Peschke, Elliott Sclar, J. Van Steenberge, *Providing Adequate Retirement Income—Pension Plans in the United States and Abroad* (Hanover, N.H.: New England Press for Brandeis University Press, 1974), Figure I.

Retirement Provision by Individuals

First, let us list some of the problems faced by an individual in preparing systematically for retirement:

1. He doesn't know with certainty when he will die.
2. He doesn't know exactly what his future income stream will be.
3. He doesn't know what his basic retirement needs will be nor what lifestyle he will ultimately prefer for that period.
4. He doesn't know when he will retire.
5. He cannot easily predict the future rate of inflation which, if it occurs, will depreciate the value of those retirement assets that do not adjust fully and reduce the buying power of income from those assets.
6. He cannot easily predict the rate of economic growth—which is likely to affect his economic position *relative* to the working population.

The number and magnitude of problems listed indicate that retirement planning is a very difficult job; the decision-making process involved in preparation for retirement (as far as the individual is concerned) is very complex. First, as listed above, the individual does not know when he's going to die. This is a major complicating factor in terms of his trying to figure out how much money he needs for retirement. To plan for adequate income the individual needs to know the number of years for which income is required. Thus arises a major justification for not providing for retirement entirely by individual mechanisms; one can simplify the decision-making process and reduce uncertainty by entering into an insurance arrangement, either public or private, that provides collective protection by grouping those who live short, medium, and long lives (discussed further in Chapter 5).

The second problem is the uncertainty of the income stream or flow the individual will receive over his working life. The problem here arises from the possibilities of such occurrences as ill health or disability (either short term or long term). More importantly, problems are created by unemployment in the labor market, job obsolescence, and unequal economic opportunity for various groups. For example, the recurrent periods of recession and inflation are outside the control of the individual and are very difficult for the individual to predict into the future. But these factors have a significant if not dominating impact on the flow of income and the total amount of income individuals receive over their lifetimes.

A third problem is the uncertainty that arises out of not knowing exactly what retirement needs will be. A major factor here is the great uncertainty that exists with regard to the state of one's health when one gets old. Will chronic or serious illness develop? Will nursing care be required? Will institutionalization be necessary? Not only does health status directly influence medical costs, it also affects retirement mobility—influencing recreation and transportation expenditures.

Additional uncertainty arises with regard to how long one's spouse will be alive. Many private retirement pensions stop or reduce payments sharply if the worker dies *before* retirement. Many pensions stop when the *retired* worker dies. Thus, the amount of money that people will need or would like to have in retirement is essentially unpredictable as far as the individual is concerned.

A fourth problem arises because of the variability in the age at which people retire. Although the individual has a large measure of control over when he retires, increasingly the decision is becoming institutionalized. This results from the growth of mandatory retirement rules, the growth of early retirement options (sometimes accompanied by management and/or union pressures to retire), and, finally, from discriminatory practices in hiring older workers.

And perhaps one of the most difficult retirement preparation problems the individual faces is the difficulty of predicting the rate of inflation that will occur *during* retirement. This problem is so very important because to the extent that the individual accumulates assets (or pension rights) for the retirement period that do not automatically adjust in value for inflation, he is faced with the prospect of these assets shrinking in value—being of little worth in the retirement period.

Finally, the individual preparing for retirement might want to be concerned about what will happen to his relative economic status in retirement. After he retires the real incomes of the working population will continue to rise over the years. If the retiree wants to keep up with the general rise in living standards, he will have to make some estimate of the growth that will occur while he is in retirement and provide additional funds for retirement that can be drawn upon to keep his economic status rising along with that of everybody else. Some people will decide that they do not want to bother dealing with the "growth" of income problem; they will be content just to keep their standard of living constant. Some may even prefer to allow it to go down. But this is an important point that should not be overlooked. There is a choice to be made, and it should not be made passively because individuals are unaware of the nature of that choice.

Required Rate of Saving for Retirement

To see the retirement preparation issues clearly, let us assume certain answers to most of the questions listed above, in order to answer the question: Suppose an individual (on his own) wants to save a sufficient amount for his retirement, how much should he save?

To put the question another way, suppose you were a preretirement counselor and someone came to you and said, "I'm twenty-five. I don't have much confidence in the present pension mechanisms available to prepare for retirement; I just don't trust them. Instead, I want to sit down and work out a savings plan for myself that will provide me with adequate income in retirement. How much should I save?"

The answer to this question depends on a great many factors. Most important are the following:

1. The standard of adequacy chosen.
2. The number of years one plans to be in retirement.
3. The number of years one plans to work and the earnings over that period.

4. The yield (if any) one can anticipate on one's savings.
5. The expected inflation that will occur over the period.

Let us look first at the standard of adequacy. The two standards described extensively in Chapter 2—the Social Security Administration's poverty index and the Bureau of Labor Statistics' Retired Couples' Budget—are possibilities. But a retirement counselor would probably argue that these are not very good standards for most people to use. Instead, it is becoming increasingly common to propose that individuals with near- or above-average incomes choose a standard of adequacy based upon the concept of "earnings replacement." An earnings-replacement standard seeks to provide the individual with income in retirement that is a certain specified percentage of his average earnings prior to retirement. Immediately, two questions arise. What should that replacement goal be; what rate should be chosen—100, 80, or 50 percent? And what period of earnings does one average to get average preretirement earnings?

For those interested, there is a whole book, *Providing Adequate Retirement Income,* devoted to looking at the above two questions. (Schulz, et al., 1974) The book develops the concept of relative income adequacy in retirement and describes innovative social security systems in Sweden, West Germany, Belgium, and Canada—countries that incorporate variations of the relative-adequacy concept into their pensions. Here we briefly summarize some of the most important points connected with providing "relative income adequacy."

What Must I Save for Adequate Retirement Income?

The amount of financial resources needed in retirement depends upon the standard of adequacy used. If the retired person's living standard is to be related in some way to a standard of living experienced before he retired, sources of retirement funds must enable him to replace a certain proportion of the income lost when work stops.

It is generally agreed that expenses in retirement will be somewhat lower than before retirement and, hence, that a 100 percent earnings replacement is not necessary. Various estimates of the differences in pre- and post-retirement expenditures have been made by different researchers. For example, the Bureau of Labor Statistics (BLS) has developed an "equivalency income scale" for families of different size and age (on the basis of the relation between food expenditures and income). BLS estimates that an elderly couple generally requires 51 percent as much income for goods and services as a younger four-person husband-wife family living on the same standard. While the BLS equivalence scale shows a difference of 51 percent in expenditures needs when comparing a *middle-aged four-person family* with an *aged couple,* the difference between couples aged 55–64 and couples aged 65 or more is much less. The scales show only a 13½ percent difference in goods and services needs.

We can use these findings to help establish a retirement living standard. This standard would *maintain the same living standard in retirement as existed just prior to retirement.* To get our estimate of the preretirement living standard we will (somewhat arbitrarily) average the earnings for *the last five years* of work before retirement.

The appropriate percentage of replacement needed can then be estimated using the BLS equivalence scale. In addition to the 13½ percent expenditure difference, one also must take into account the reduced income tax burden in retirement due to the current federal income tax law's special provisions for persons aged 65 and over. Also, presumably the individual upon reaching retirement can discontinue saving for retirement, a requirement that reduces his disposable income in the working years. Taking these three factors into account, the appropriate replacement is about 60–65 percent of *gross* income for a middle income worker.

One can now calculate (using certain assumptions) the saving rate necessary to achieve a specified living standard in retirement. That is, one can determine what amount must be saved every year out of earnings up to the point of retirement. The year one begins saving is arbitrary. One could decide to start saving at, say, age 25, or one could decide to postpone the task till age 45 and then save more over a shorter period.

Let us assume, for example, that one begins to save a certain percent of annual income *starting the first year of work* and that one saves the *same proportion* of earnings throughout one's whole lifetime. Assume a life expectancy equal to the current average life expectancy. Assume retirement at age 65. Assume an investment return on savings of 4 percent.

Suppose one's goal is to provide retirement income equal to 60–65 percent replacement of average earnings during the last five years prior to retirement. *To do this, one would have to save about 20 percent of one's earnings each and every year!**

*A full description of how this estimate was made can be found in Schulz and Carrin (1972).

An individual might desire, however, to save at a lower rate in the earlier years when earnings are relatively low compared to anticipated earnings later in his career. In such a case, later savings rates would have to be much higher and disposable income in the years prior to retirement would be lower.

In addition, the question of child-rearing expenses arises. A family with children has a lower standard of living than a family without children but with a similar income. Once a couple's children are self-supporting, the couple's standard of living may rise as a result of the reduced expenditures of this sort. Whether this occurs depends in part on whether the family has incurred previous debts—arising, for example, from educational or unusual medical expenses. Paying off these debts might prevent any significant increase in living standards in the preretirement years.

The Introduction of Social Security and Private Pensions

The required saving rate of about 20 percent presented in the preceding section assumed that one saved for retirement without the help of either public or private pension plans. However, public and private pension plans do exist and are growing; we have some evidence, also, that these plans influence the saving decisions of individuals. Thus, in the case of public pensions, the magnitude of the individual's job in preparing for retirement by saving is partly reduced because of benefits rights acquired through his payments to the social security system. But we should not forget that the substitution of pensions for individual savings also results in the institution of payroll taxes (social security) and lower take-home pay (private pensions). Somebody has to pay for the group benefits.

Different required savings rates can be computed that take into account social security old-age pensions. In the past few years social security pensions in the United States have been increased a great deal, the largest single increase occurring in 1972. Table 15 contrasts the required savings rates for three cases: the rates required without social security; the rates required, given social security pensions based on the 1969 formula; and, finally, the rates of saving required as a result of pensions based on the 1972 social security formula. The table shows the very large drop in required savings rates as a result of introducing and improving public pensions.

Table 15   Alternative Required Saving Rates, by Percent

Living Standard	Without Social Security	With Social Security	
		1969 Formula	*1972 Formula*
Replacement of 60–65 Percent of Preretirement Average Earnings	20.5	11.3	5.5

Source: James H. Schulz, et al., *Providing Adequate Retirement Income—Pension Reform in the United States and Abroad* (Hanover, N.H.: New England Press for Brandeis University Press, 1974).

The required savings rates presented above help explain why past generations of older Americans (and many of the current elderly) found themselves in such a relatively poor economic condition. Average personal savings rates in the United States have remained relatively constant over the years and have not equaled by far the rates required to provide adequate funds in retirement. Moreover, *average* rates of saving are an aggregation of the differing rates for many individuals—most of whom save at rates below the average. The introduction of social security in the late thirties provided the aged with benefits that satisfied only a very minimal adequacy standard. At the same time, personal savings rates have generally been at rates below those required to provide sufficient supplementation to raise the retirement funds to a more acceptable standard of adequacy. Moreover, the introduction of private pension plans, which grew rapidly in the forties and fifties, did not have a significant impact on the economic situation of the many aged who retired without such coverage.

Future Saving Adequacy

Having looked at required rates of saving, it would be appropriate to give some attention to the current saving behavior of individuals and how it might change in the future. In the past, surveys of the aged have shown that the assets of older people are concentrated in the hands of a minority of the aged population. As we saw in Chapter 2, statistics indicate that many people reach old age with little or no savings. In fact, a very large proportion of them reach old age with little or no *liquid* assets. Most of the savings of older people in the lower- and middle-income groups is in the form of home equity.

One can argue that this situation will change in the future. It is sometimes predicted that future saving behavior will change and that people are now better able to save for their old age as a result of the higher earnings and higher living standard associated with the so-called "affluent society." For example, in *Capitalism and Freedom* (University of Chicago Press, 1962) economist Milton Friedman argues that the social security system was instituted during the period of the thirties when there were large numbers of people unemployed, when incomes were very low, and when there were large numbers of older people living in poverty. These conditions triggered the demand for social legislation to do something for these people. Friedman argues that present conditions do not justify the continuation of such programs, since they were designed for the conditions at those times, which do not exist at present.

Unfortunately, if we try to assess arguments of this type made by Friedman and others, we find that the data on saving behavior of individuals and asset accumulation are not very good.*

Data from the Social Security Administration's Retirement History Study, however, provide 1969 asset statistics for a cohort of individuals approaching retirement. Table 16 contrasts the financial asset situation of the 1967 aged population with the asset picture for "preaged" persons age 58 to 63 in 1969. The data show that there has been little improvement in the financial asset status of this preretirement group as compared to the current elderly. In fact, the two distributions are almost identical.

Also included in Table 16, to provide some historical perspective, is the financial asset situation for the elderly five years earlier (1962). Again, the data show that the distribution in that year is virtually identical with the 1967 situation.

Inflation and Saving

Some people have argued that saving, particularly personal saving, is discouraged by the uncertainty of not knowing the rate of inflation. Another way of saying this is that people are discouraged from saving by the certainty of knowing that inflation is bound to take place at some rate and that their savings are likely to become devalued over time.

The form in which savings are held determines the impact of inflation on accumulated wealth. Historically, some assets have adjusted

*The most recent study is by Goldstein (1965). The study analyzes data from the U.S. Bureau of Labor Statistics' Consumer Expenditure surveys. Unfortunately, it is recognized that the saving information collected in these surveys is very unreliable.

Table 16   Financial Assets[a] of the Aged and a "Preretirement" Cohort, by Percent

Asset Amount	Survey Units with Head Age 58–63 in 1969[b]	Survey Units with Head Age 65 or More in 1967[b]	Survey Units with Head Age 65 or More in 1962
None	25	36	35
$1–999	22	19	19
$1000–2999	14	12	12
$3000–4999	7	7	7
$5000–9999	10	10	9
$10,999–19,999	9	8 }	18
$20,000 or More	12	8 }	
Total Percent	100[c]	100	100

Source: Based on data in Janet Murray, "Homeownership and Financial Assets: Findings from the 1968 Survey of the Aged," *Social Security Bulletin* (August 1972): 3–23; Sally R. Sherman, "Assets on the Threshold of Retirement," *Social Security Bulletin* (August 1973): 3–17; and Lenore A. Epstein and Janet H. Murray, *The Aged Population of the United States,* Office of Research and Statistics Research Report No. 19 (Washington, D.C.: U.S. Government Printing Office, 1967).
[a]U.S. savings bonds, checking accounts, savings accounts, stocks, corporate bonds, mutual funds, and money owed by others.
[b]Tabulation of married couples and nonmarried individuals.
[c]Does not add up to 100 due to rounding.

very poorly, primarily because of relatively fixed rates of return: bank deposits, insurance contracts, and bonds. Others, which have adjusted better, require considerable financial sophistication or have much higher associated risk: real estate, corporate stock, and gold.

Various proposals have been made for the creation of a different type of financial asset, a constant purchasing power bond. These bonds would be sold by the government to people to protect their savings from inflation.

The basic idea of constant purchasing power bonds is that people should be able to buy these bonds from the government to save for retirement or other purposes. They might or might not receive interest from them. Economist James Tobin has argued, for example, that people might even be willing to buy these bonds at a zero rate of interest—as long as there was a firm guarantee that their value would not depreciate from inflation.

Having been purchased for a stated amount, the bond would be redeemable at some point in the future for that amount, *adjusted for any inflation that took place over the intervening period*. Thus, the value of the bond would remain constant in real terms and actually increase if there was a rate of interest associated with it.

Henry Wallich (1969), himself an advocate of the bonds, summarizes the *opposition* to them as follows:

> The case against purchasing power bonds every good official can recite in his sleep. If you escalate government obligations, people will say that you are throwing in the towel against inflation. Investors will stop worrying about inflation if they are protected. And the government with its unlimited resources would be competing unfairly with private borrowers who could not take the risk of assuming this kind of open-ended debt.

Milton Friedman (1971) argues against this sort of reasoning:

> The government alone is responsible for inflation. By inflation it has expropriated the capital of persons who bought government securities. Often at the urging of high officials who eloquently proclaimed that patriotism and self-interest went hand-in-hand (the good old government savings bond). The right way to avoid this disgraceful shell game is for the government to borrow in the form of purchasing power securities. Let the Treasury promise to pay not $1000, but a sum that will have the same purchasing power as $1000 had when the security was issued. Let it pay as interest each year not a fixed amount of dollars but that number adjusted for any rise in prices. This would be the precise counterpart of the escalator clauses that have become so popular in wage contracts.

The late Senator Pat McNamara from Michigan, when he was chairman of the Special Committee on Aging, introduced legislation in the early sixties to allow the government to sell purchasing power bonds to individuals up to a certain maximum amount, on the condition that the individuals would be willing to hold the bonds until retirement. The proposed legislation specified that if the bonds were cashed in before retirement, there would not be an escalator adjustment; instead, individuals would only get back the original amount plus a stipulated amount of interest. Senator McNamara introduced the bill over a period of many years, but hearings were never held on the proposal.

The principal opposition to purchasing power bonds is centered in the U.S. Treasury Department. In addition to the reasons cited by Wallich (see above), the Treasury worries about possible destabilizing effects on the bond markets of introducing this new type of bond and the possibility of making more difficult the government's debt financing. In this particular area—debt management and federal debt issue—the Treasury is politically very powerful. Thus far, it has been persuasive in preventing the Congress from seriously considering legislation of this sort.

We will return to the question of protecting the real value of savings later in the book. One of the proposals for reforming social security we discuss in Chapter 8 is the Buchanan plan for compulsory saving through private and public retirement bonds indexed to adjust, at a minimum, for inflation.

Suggested Readings

The American Enterprise Institute. *Indexing and Inflation*. Washington, D.C.: The American Enterprise Institute, 1974.

  A round-table discussion by economists Milton Friedman, Robert J. Gordon, William Fellner, and former Deputy Secretary of the Treasury Charles Walker presenting arguments for and against indexing.

Kreps, Juanita. "The Economy and the Aged." In Robert H. Binstock and Ethel Shanas, eds. *The Handbook of Aging and the Social Sciences*. New York: Van Nostrand Reinhold, 1976.

  This includes a good review of the literature regarding growth and economic fluctuations as they affect the aged's economic position. Also discussed is the interrelation among education, productivity, and lifetime earnings.

Munnell, Alicia H. *The Effect of Social Security on Personal Saving*. Cambridge, Mass.: Ballinger, 1974.

  A statistical analysis of the issue. Also, this book contains a reanalysis (and new results) of data from a prior well-known study investigating the impact of private pensions on personal saving by Philip Cagan.

Schulz, James H., et al. *Providing Adequate Retirement Income—Pension Reform in the United States and Abroad*. Hanover, N.H.: New England Press for Brandeis University Press, 1974.

  This book presents a more extensive treatment of the topics in this chapter. It emphasizes the replacement of average preretirement earnings by pensions as a measure of adequacy. Innovative pension systems in five countries are analyzed.

Chapter Five

The Role of Pensions

The Great Depression of the 1930's went a long way toward exposing the great political lie of American welfare debates: that poverty was generally the result of the laziness or personal unworthiness of particular individuals. In the thirties it became painfully obvious to everyone that this was not the case. Millions of jobless workers and their families suffered severe financial problems because of an economic catastrophe caused by factors unrelated to their own personal activities. Moreover, the cures for their problems lay almost entirely outside the range of their individual reactions.

Up until this depression there had been a great deal of controversy in the United States with regard to the role of (and need for) some sort of public pension system. Many other countries had quickly followed the example of Germany, which established the first comprehensive social insurance program in the 1880's. But in the United States there was no widespread public support for public pensions until the economic upheavals of the Great Depression. And, although there was a scattered handful of employee pensions provided by government and private firms in existence during the first half of the twentieth century, the significant growth of these pension programs has occurred in the relatively recent years of the 1950's and 1960's.

Thus, the social institution of "pensions" has had a relatively short history in the United States. And there has been continuing discussion and debate over just what are the appropriate roles to be played by both public and private pensions.

In this chapter we look at this question and discuss some of the important goals for a good pension program; in the next chapters we look at social security and private pensions as they currently operate in the United States.

Why Pensions?

While some of the debate over pensions has centered around the advantages and disadvantages of public versus private pensions, there are two even more basic questions that should be discussed: Why is there a need for *any kind* of pension program? And should individuals be compelled (either by the government or an employer) to join a particular pension program?

You will recall that in Chapter 4 we listed and discussed a number of problems confronting an individual who wishes to make economic preparations for retirement on his own. The first problem is that the individual does not know exactly when he or she will die, that is, how long a period to provide for. This means that any person or family preparing for retirement must assume the "worst"—a long life—and put aside enough money to take care of that eventuality; or must be prepared to rely on private or public charity if they live "too long" and their own economic support is exhausted.

A pension program provides an attractive option by utilizing a basic insurance principle. If the number of individuals in a pension program is sufficiently large, mortality tables of life expectancy can be constructed that estimate average life expectancy at particular ages. Retirement preparation costs can then be geared to *average* life expectancy, with the "excess" payments of individuals who die before the average age going to those who live beyond it. The result is that no one has to pay more than he or she would need to personally put aside if it was known with certainty that he or she would live for a period of years equal to the average life expectancy.

The second problem discussed in Chapter 4 in connection with individual retirement preparation is the lack of predictability of future income. For example, chronic low earnings, ill health, or becoming unemployed as a result of a variety of factors may make sufficient saving for retirement very difficult or even impossible. Also, health or employment problems may force an individual to leave the labor force unexpectedly and much earlier than was originally planned.

Collective arrangements to deal with this problem are not new. People since earliest times have attempted to mitigate or eliminate economic insecurity by banding together in groups—families, tribes, associations, guilds. Especially important has been the family. Throughout history individuals have relied heavily on family ties to protect themselves from economic insecurity in old age. Even today in the United States, the family remains an important source of economic and social support for many older persons. And in some other countries—particularly those less industrialized—the family still remains the major source of economic protection and security in old age.

The major problem with the family (and many other group associations) for sharing risk is that the number of people involved is relatively small. As Kenneth Boulding (1958) has observed, "It is when the 'sharing group' becomes too small to ensure that there will always be enough producers in it to support the unproductive that devices for insurance become necessary. When the 'sharing group' is small there is always a danger that sheer accident will bring the proportion of earners to nonearners to a level at which the group cannot function."

The commonly held view that in earlier America most of the aged lived in rural communities together with or in close proximity to adult children who provided financial support in the later years is not supported by the facts. (Tibbitts, 1960) Nuclear parent-child families have always been the more common family type in the United States, and the three-generation family has been relatively rare.

Thus, the need for better collective arrangements to deal with the economic problems of old age has probably always been with us. The earliest available statistics on the economic status of the elderly prior to the establishment of pensions indicate that most of the aged were poor and that, in fact, many were completely destitute. The reasons why pension programs were not developed sooner are not entirely clear, but various writers have pointed to the *relative* economic prosperity throughout America's history, the country's decentralized governmental structure, and (most importantly) the individualistic ethic of much of the population.

But if pensions are a useful way of providing economic security in old age, should participation be compulsory?

Why Compulsory Pensions?

Although individual self-reliance and voluntary preparation for retirement—together with family interdependence—dominated the early discussions of old-age security provision, it is now generally accepted that this is not the appropriate cornerstone of an income-maintenance policy for the aged. Instead, there is widespread support for relying on compulsory pensions.

A number of prominent American economists have written about the rationale for compulsory pensions. In a chapter in his book on the *Principles of Economic Policy*, Kenneth Boulding (1958) concisely states the principal argument:

> [If an individual were] rationally motivated, [he] would be aware of the evils that might beset him, and would insure against them. It is argued, however, that many people are not so motivated, and that hardly anyone is completely motivated by these rational considerations, and that therefore under a purely voluntary system some will insure and some will not. This means, however, that those who do not insure will have to be supported anyway—perhaps at lower levels and in humiliating and respect-destroying ways—when they are in the nonproductive phase of life, but that they will escape the burden of paying premiums when they are in the productive phase. In fairness to those who insure voluntarily, and in order to maintain the self-respect of those who would not otherwise insure, insurance should be compulsory.

Richard Musgrave (1968), writing on the role of social insurance, makes a similar point:

> Insurance could be purchased privately, but becomes a matter of public concern only because [some] will not do so, while [others] will. Given their humanitarian premise, Calvin and Homer must bail out Jack should the contingency arise. They will require therefore that Jack should insure. Social insurance is now insurance in the technical sense, but its basic function (and especially the rationale for making it mandatory) is again to avoid burdening the prudent.

And finally Pechman, Aaron, and Taussig (1968) in their book on social security, after an extensive discussion of the rationale for pensions, conclude:

> There is widespread myopia with respect to retirement needs. Empirical evidence shows that most people fail to save enough to prevent catastrophic drops in postretirement income.... Not only do people fail to plan ahead carefully for retirement; even in the later years of their working life, many remain unaware of impending retirement needs.... In an urban, industrial society, government intervention in the saving-consumption decision is needed to implement personal preferences over the life cycle. *There is nothing inconsistent in the decision to undertake through the political process a course of action which would not be undertaken individually through the market place.* [Emphasis added.]

J. Douglas Brown, who helped draft the original social security program, writes in his book on the history of social security that the drafting group never seriously considered anything other than a compulsory program. The drafting group did worry, however, about whether a national, compulsory program would be constitutional.

Hoping that it might be possible to avoid a court test of the constiutionality of social security, the drafting group did consider briefly a plan that would have permitted elective social security coverage by states and various industrial groups but rejected it. According to Brown, the plan was "so cumbersome, ineffective, and actuarially unsound that no further attempt was made to avoid a head-on constitutional test of a truly workable system." (Brown, 1972)

As it turned out, during the debates that followed, the principal argument for compulsion was a financing one. It was argued that an optional coverage program would make it actuarially impossible to project both benefits (costs) and revenue. It was feared that this problem would create financial instability and make it difficult to guarantee adequate, equitable, and improved benefits as social security developed.

The original Social Security Act required participation by all workers in commerce and industry except those working for railroads.* A number of groups, however, were specifically excluded from coverage—the major ones being farm workers, the self-employed, and government employees (including military personnel). Over the years, as coverage was extended to these groups, optional coverage was introduced for certain specific groups: employees of nonprofit institutions, state and local governments, and most clergymen. But in each case, coverage was not optional for the individual, depending instead on the collective decision of the organizational unit.

The decision of the United States to have a compulsory pension program is in no way unique. There is no country in the world with a social security old-age pension program that has designed a large amount of voluntary coverage into the program. Like the United States, many countries have special public pension programs for certain groups of workers (especially government employees), and many exclude from coverage certain groups (such as farm workers, the self-employed, or employees of very small firms). Currently only a few countries—Ghana, the Federal Republic of Germany, Mali, Taiwan, the United Kingdom, and Zambia—have any voluntary coverage, and these noncompulsory provisions are all limited to certain (usually small) groups.

---

*Railroad workers were exempted because similar legislation on their behalf had already been enacted in 1934. Although this original legislation was later declared unconstitutional, new (and still separate) railroad pension legislation was enacted in 1935 and 1937.

If we shift our attention from public pensions to private pensions in the United States, we find that the situation is not very different. The vast majority of workers who are covered or not covered by private pension plans have not achieved that status by personal election. Not all firms have established private pension plans for their employees, but almost all private pension schemes that have been set up are compulsory. Typically, once a worker joins a firm he automatically becomes a member of the pension plan—sometimes after a short waiting period. There are a few private plans, however, that provide for an employee contribution out of salary; such plans sometimes make coverage optional.

In summary, we see that the usefulness of pensions in helping to provide for economic security in old age is generally accepted and that compulsory coverage remains a feature of both public and private programs.

What Makes a "Good" Pension Program?

If one wants to evaluate a pension program or a pension proposal, what characteristics or features of the plan should be examined? With an institutional arrangement as complex as pensions, one can generate a long list of plan features that might be studied. Opinions differ widely as to which of these are most important. Moreover, there is little agreement among various people on the relative weights that should be assigned to each feature when making an overall judgment about whether a particular pension plan is good or bad. Some important characteristics of pension plans, however, that would probably appear on almost everyone's list, are the following:

The Adequacy of Pension Benefits   Any discussion of a particular pension plan's benefit adequacy must explicitly recognize the variety of means available to the individual (or society) in achieving a particular level of income in old age. A pension plan is rarely designed to be the sole source of such income. Thus, in evaluating the adequacy of any particular pension benefit, it is necessary to relate such analysis to a general framework for evaluating individuals' general economic status and the variety of means available to achieve or change that status. Are individuals *expected* to accumulate personal savings for their old age? Are all individuals *able* to save for old age? What noncash programs (such as health insurance) are available to provide economic support?

How large are both public and private pension benefits; who is currently covered by each; who should be covered?

There will never be complete agreement about the appropriate roles for the various means of providing income in old age—collective pensions schemes being only one major way (see Figure 8, page 68). Rather, it is almost certain that there will be continuing political debate and private discussion among bargaining groups over these matters. Out of such discussions come decisions on legislation, employment contracts, and employer policies in the area of pensions. As these decisions are made, it is possible to evaluate their economic implications for retirement-income adequacy, estimating the contribution the resulting pensions will make to a particular individual's or group's income-adequacy goal.

The Certainty of Benefits   In addition to estimating or projecting the size of pension benefits, one can examine particular pension plans and estimate the degree of uncertainty associated with the *promised* benefits. Three major contingencies can be evaluated:

1. Plan termination: what provisions are made to ensure that the plan will survive economic or political adversity, such as a change in government (public pensions) or bankruptcy of the firm (private pensions)?
2. Inflation: how well are the workers' future benefits and the pension recipients' actual benefits protected from general increases in the level of prices?
3. Job termination: what happens to pension rights if a worker involuntarily or by choice stops working or changes jobs?

Flexibility and Discretion for Varying Conditions or Preferences   The larger the pension program in terms of people covered, the greater the differences in the circumstances and preferences of these participants. It is generally desirable for pension plan provisions and rules not to be too rigid. The introduction of greater flexibility, however, usually results in greater administrative costs (see Low Administrative Costs, below). And by complicating the program, flexibility often makes it more difficult for participants to become knowledgeable and to understand "their" pension program.

Adequate and Nondiscriminatory Coverage   The determination of eligibility for pension coverage is a very complex but important factor in assessing pension plans. Most people would agree that individuals in similar circumstances (e.g., working for the same employer) should not be arbitrarily exluded from coverage under a pension plan or excluded because of age, sex, race, etc. But the actual determination of who should and who should not be included is often difficult because of a variety of administrative, technical, political, and economic considerations.

Equity   Whether a pension program is perceived as being "fair" depends in large measure on how the program treats different individuals and how these individuals think they *should* be treated. The major issue around which equity questions usually center is financing—how much do the benefits received cost the individual in contrast to other benefit recipients and possibly nonrecipients? Chapter 8 of this book is devoted to financing pensions and a discussion of some of the most important equity questions.

Low Administrative Costs   Apart from the benefits paid out by a pension program, there are a variety of expenditures connected with keeping records, determining benefit eligibility, collecting and managing the funds used to pay benefits, and informing individuals of their rights under the plan.

Boulding (1958) has argued that one valid criterion for choosing between private versus public programs is whether there can be significant economies of scale in their operation. "If there are these economies—that is, if the cost of administering the insurance declines with every increase in the amount of insurance written—then a state monopoly will almost inevitably be cheaper than a number of competing private companies.... We may venture a hypothesis that where the operations of insurance are fairly routine, the case for state or national monopoly is stronger than where the operations involve great difficulties of definition of rights."

Simplicity and Ease of Understanding   It is important that individuals know whether they are covered by a pension plan, what the conditions of entitlement are, what benefits they (or their family) can or will receive, what the risks of losing benefits are, and various other information about the plan. Over the years a large amount of evidence has accumulated that indicates a great lack of knowledge and misinformation exists among workers in the United States with regard to their own expected pensions, both public and private. As the number and variety of pension programs grow and many of these programs become more complicated, this problem will also grow. Therefore, in reviewing existing programs or proposals for pension changes, consideration should be given to the complexity of the program. An assessment should be made of the resultant impact on the employees' ability to understand the pension program and to realistically incorporate it into their pre-retirement planning.

Integration Pensions are almost always only one of a number of collective programs operating to provide economic assistance. It is not sufficient to view a particular pension program isolated from these other programs. For example, eligibility or benefit determination under one program is sometimes related to benefits received from another program.

This is an especially important issue with regard to public programs. The value of social security pension benefits to the elderly depends, for example, on (a) the tax treatment of these benefits, and (b) whether the benefits are counted as income in determining eligibility for Supplemental Security Income, food stamps, Medicare and Medicaid, housing subsidies, etc. (*See*, for example, Federal Council on Aging, 1975)

Suggested Readings

Boulding, Kenneth. "Income Maintenance Policy." Chapter 10 in *Principles of Economic Policy*. Englewood Cliffs, N.J.: Prentice Hall, 1958, pp. 233-257.
> One of the best discussions of the rationale for pension insurance and one of the few discussions available on the relative merits of public versus private pensions.

Friedman, Milton. *Capitalism and Freedom*. Chicago: University of Chicago Press, 1962.
> Arguments are presented in Chapter 11 against compulsory pensions.

Turnbull, John G.; C. Arthur Williams, Jr.; and Earl F. Cheit. *Economic and Social Security*. 4th ed. New York: Ronald Press, 1973.
> A number of the early chapters discuss various concepts of pension insurance and the differences between public and private insurance.

Viscusi, Wikip, and Richard Zeckhauser. *Welfare of the Elderly*. New York: Wiley Interscience, 1976.
> Various chapters discuss how best to provide economic welfare for older people. See especially Chapter 10, "Collective Savings Schemes—Social Security and Pensions."

Wilensky, Harold L. *The Welfare State and Equality: The Structural and Ideological Roots of Public Expenditures*. Berkeley: University of California Press, 1975.
> Wilensky attempts to investigate empirically how ideology, politics, and the economy affect the development of the welfare state. The book presents evidence indicating that the level of economic development is the most important factor influencing the level of welfare programs, including pensions.

Chapter Six

Social Security

The first American social security benefit ever paid was $22 a month and was received by Miss Ida Fuller, a retired law firm secretary, in early 1940. Ida Fuller's experience with social security dramatically illustrates one of the major benefits of public pensions discussed in the prior chapter. Miss Fuller (who died in 1975) lived to be over a hundred, paid into the program less than $100, and over the years received more than $20,000 in social security benefits.*

In response to the needs of Ida Fuller and millions of other persons approaching retirement, the United States social security system was created in 1935 and has grown over the years to be one of the major expenditure programs of the federal government.

The Social Security Act of 1935 established a federal old-age pension program (OAI) and a federal-state system of unemployment insurance. In 1939 survivors' benefits were added (OASI). In 1956 social security was expanded to include disability insurance to protect severely disabled workers (OASDI). In 1965 Medicare was added, establishing a comprehensive health program for the elderly (OASDHI). Over the period of 1950–67, successive groups of workers were brought into the system: certain farm and domestic workers (1950), most self-employed (1954), members of the uniformed services (1956), Americans employed

---

*As we discuss in Chapter 8, one of the reasons why many people like Ida Fuller receive significantly more benefits than the contributions they paid into the program is because Congress decided to reduce the eligibility requirements (i.e., the work/payment period) for older workers approaching retirement when the program was first established (and later when new groups were brought into the program). Of course, the fact that Ida Fuller lived far beyond the average life expectancy also raised her benefits relative to her contributions.

by foreign governments or international organizations (1960), physicians (1965), and ministers (1967). Finally in 1972 the railroad retirement program was integrated with the social security system.*

Total annual OASDHI expenditures have grown from less than $1 billion in 1950 to $78.5 billion in 1975. This chapter focuses primarily on the social security old-age pension program (OASI). The pension discussion is mainly about benefits, however, since financing is discussed extensively in Chapter 8. At the end of the chapter we briefly discuss disability programs, public medical insurance, and the Supplemental Security Income program.

The Changing Social Security System

Paradoxically, the major motivating force behind the passage of the Social Security Act in 1935 was not the provision of adequate income in retirement but the creation of jobs. Passed in a period that at one point witnessed more than a quarter of the labor force without jobs, the social security legislation was one of many New Deal laws aimed at job creation and relief for those out of work. The 1935 legislation encouraged the creation of state-administered unemployment programs to help unemployed workers find work and to provide them with financial support while they looked. Old-age pensions were provided to help the elderly financially but also *to encourage them to leave or remain out of the work force.* Old-age benefits to otherwise eligible persons age 65 or over were made conditional on meeting a "retirement test." In the original 1935 act, benefits were *not* to be paid to persons receiving any "covered wages from regular employment."

Regular employment, however, was not specifically defined in the 1935 act. In the 1939 social security amendments, the retirement test was made less ambiguous by language that specified that no benefits would be paid to anyone earning more than $14.99 a month in covered employment.

Over the years the earnings exemption was increased periodically by specific increments. In 1972, the exemption amount or retire-

*We do not discuss the railroad retirement system in this book. Those interested in recent developments should read Alfred M. Skolnik, "Restructuring the Railroad Retirement System," *Social Security Bulletin* 38 (April 1975): 23-29.

ment test was set at $2100 (effective January 1973), to be automatically adjusted upward along with the rise in average earnings (with benefits reduced by 50 percent of earnings *above* the exempt amount). By 1976 the exempt amount had reached $2760.

Over the past three and a half decades there have been a great many changes in the social security system. Except for the introduction of disability insurance in 1956 and medical insurance (Medicare) in 1965, however, there have been few, if any, *major* changes, although two historical developments are of particular interest. First, as a result of a series of legislated liberalizations, there was an expansion of persons covered by the system. Currently the only major groups of gainfully employed workers not covered are (a) federal civilian employees and certain state and local government employees with other pension coverage, (b) farm and domestic workers who do not earn or work "enough," and (c) self-employed persons with very low net earnings. Second, legislation over the years has gradually moved the system further away from financing procedures that would result in the creation of a large monetary reserve fund.

While pension financing will be discussed in Chapter 8, some initial remarks are appropriate here. Currently the social security system is almost completely "unfunded" (i.e., few reserves are accumulated and obligations are met essentially on a pay-as-you-go basis). From the very beginning social security was never completely funded. It was recognized from the start that this was not necessary since mandatory participation resulted in the number of participants being a large part of the employed population, since the pension system could be assumed to operate indefinitely, and since the taxing power of the government ultimately stands behind the system.

Initially, legislated contribution rates were expected to provide the money for a fairly large trust fund as payments came in over the years. But as this reserve fund began to accumulate and actuarial projections predicted that it would grow much bigger, congressional leaders began to argue that there was no reason for the fund to grow so big. Instead, the decision was made to liberalize the system and to use the scheduled increases in contributions to pay for these liberalizations.

Historically, the gradual adoption of an almost completely pay-as-you-go funding policy served to facilitate the liberalization and improvement of the system. New groups were added to the system with the provision of benefits retroactively. Cost-of-living increases in benefits were legislated periodically. And, in 1972, a major increase in real benefits was provided for everyone in the system.

The Principles of Social Security

The social security legislation that was accepted by President Roosevelt and the Congress had a number of basic principles built into it:

First, for the designated groups participation was compulsory. Workers could not opt out of the system. Nor were high-income or high-earnings members of the covered groups excluded.

Second, it was set up as an earnings-related system. When this decision was made in the 1930's, it was not at all obvious that social security should be based upon an earnings-related principle. Many countries in Europe had flat-rate pensions. And Dr. Francis E. Townsend, a California physician, had proposed in 1933 a flat pension of $200 per month for all persons aged 60 and over—resulting in the "Townsend movement" of 4550 clubs within two years.

The decision was made not to go in that direction. J. Douglas Brown, one of the architects of the system, writes that "it was early recognized that a single flat rate of benefits for a country as diversified as the United States would fail to meet the needs of those living in the high-cost urban areas of the Northeast while being unduly favorable to those in the rural South."

Third, it was decided that social security should be only one of many sources of economic protection and that further supplementation, either through group or individual means, would be necessary in order to maintain an adequate living standard in retirement. Social security was often referred to as providing "a floor of protection."

Fourth, social security benefits were to be a matter of right; there was to be no means test. Workers were to earn their benefits through participation in and contributions to the program. The system was to be self-supporting through these worker contributions together with so-called "employer contributions."*

Fifth, "social adequacy" was to be taken into account in the determination of benefits for various recipients. A set of weighted benefits that favored workers with lower earnings was established. Also, a contribution cutoff point (the maximum contribution ceiling) was established; the earnings above the ceiling of very highly paid earners were excluded. The intent was to restrict the focus of the program to those people who would have the greatest problems and the greatest need for a public benefit (while allowing all eligible earners to participate).

*We discuss in Chapter 8 the question of who actually pays the employer contribution—the employee through reduced wages, consumers through higher prices, or the firm itself.

Sixth, as indicated above, a "retirement test" was established; pension benefits were to be withheld, initially, if an age-eligible person worked and eventually if a person earned above a specified amount.

Retirement Benefit Provisions*

Benefits paid under the old-age and survivors' insurance program to workers and their spouses can be broken down into the following components:

1. The BASIC BENEFIT, paid at age 65, is based upon the worker's average monthly earnings below the "earnings ceiling" in covered employment and is derived from a legislated benefit formula that is weighted to provide workers with lower "average earnings" a relatively greater percentage of earnings replacement than workers with higher earnings. Benefits are limited by the ceiling placed on the earnings upon which a worker previously paid contributions. Only taxed earnings below this ceiling enter into the calculation of the average monthly earnings used in the benefit formula. Also, total family benefits are limited by a maximum amount.
2. A MINIMUM BENEFIT is provided workers (and survivors) who would otherwise be eligible for very low basic benefits. A special minimum benefit (which is larger) is payable to persons with 20 or more years of covered employment, the size being dependent on the number of years of covered employment between 20 and 30.
3. A DEPENDENT BENEFIT, equal to 50 percent of the worker's basic benefit, may be paid to a wife and children under age 18 (and those age 18 to 21 if full time students). Disabled children, husbands, and divorced wives may also receive a benefit if certain specified conditions are met.
4. EARLY RETIREMENT BENEFITS may be paid to beneficiaries at age 62–64, but these benefits are actuarially reduced to take into account the longer period over which they will be paid.
5. DELAYED BENEFITS are paid to workers who claim their pension beyond age 65. An additional 1 percent is added to their benefits for each year (after 1970) between ages 65 and 72 that they do not get benefits.
6. A RETIREMENT TEST reduces benefits paid persons under age 72 (and their dependents) who earn more than a certain amount. Benefits are reduced one dollar for every two dollars earned above the

*The disability program is not discussed until later in this chapter. Some students of social security, however, see it as an important part of a *retirement* program, providing transitional protection for many of those unable to continue working up to the OASI eligibility ages. See Chapter 9 (page 160) for a discussion of this issue.

exempt amount. The exemption ($2760 in 1976) increases auto-
matically with increases in the Consumer Price Index.

7. SURVIVORS' BENEFITS are payable to a surviving wife
beginning at age 60 or, if disabled, at age 50, or, if there is a
dependent child (under 18 or disabled), at any age. This benefit
equals 100 percent of the basic benefit (see 1. above) for widows age
65 or over and disabled widows age 60 or over. Reduced benefits are
paid to widows age 60–64 and to disabled widows age 50–59. Unmarried and disabled children, dependent parents, divorced wives,
widowers and remarried widows are also eligible for survivors'
benefits when meeting certain specified conditions.

Each of these components of the social security program are discussed in
more detail below.

Benefit Levels   One of the best ways of evaluating the level of
pension benefits being paid is to look at "pension replacement rates."
You will remember from Chapter 4 that pension replacement rates
specify the proportion of a worker's prior earnings that are replaced by
the pension he receives.

Data from the Social Security Administration's Survey of New
Beneficiaries provide us with the only available comprehensive information on the amount of earnings replaced (in the recent past) by public and
private pensions. A Social Security Administration study (Fox, 1974) reports on the pension replacement rates achieved by social security recipients retiring in 1970. Table 17 presents an updating of this earlier
study, listing the median percent of total earnings replaced by social
security for four groups retiring in 1970 and 1974.

In 1974 the median social security pension replacement rates
varied between 29 and 47 percent. Workers with earnings below the
social security maximum taxable earnings level had higher replacement
rates, principally because of the weighted benefit formula, which favors
low earnings. *Workers with earnings above the maximum received pensions that replaced only about one-quarter of their preretirement average
earnings.*

While the Social Security Administration study provides important and very useful replacement data, it suffers from two major limitations. The most important one is that no earnings-replacement rates are
available for families. The pension amounts reported in Table 17, for example, do not include any spouse benfits. But for many purposes, it
would be useful to know the ratio of total family pension income to total
average family earnings. Also, estimates of replacement rates using after-
tax earnings would be very useful.

Table 17 Percent of Total Estimated[a] Earnings Replaced by Social Security,[b] 1970 and 1974 Retirees[c]

	Median Percent	
	1970	1974
Men with earnings[d] *below* the social security maximum	36	44
Women with earnings[d] *below* the social security maximum .	40	47
Men with earnings *above*[e] the social security maximum	23	29
Women with earnings *above*[e] the social security maximum. .	25	31

Source: Alan Fox, *Earnings Replacement from Social Security and Private Pensions: Newly Entitled Beneficiaries, 1970.* Preliminary Findings from the Survey of New Beneficiaries, Report No. 13 (Washington, D.C.: Office of Research and Statistics, U.S. Social Security Administration, 1974) and Alan Fox, *Earnings Replacement from Social Security Benefits: Newly Entitled Beneficiaries, 1974.* Research and Statistics Note (Washington, D.C.: Office of Research and Statistics, U.S. Social Security Administration, forthcoming).
[a]The measure uses a crude estimation of total earnings for those workers whose reported earnings were equal to or greater than the social security taxable maximum in any of the three highest years.
[b]Old-age pension benefits *excluding* any spouse benefit.
[c]Persons newly entitled to benefits payable at award (January to June 1970 awards and July to December 1974 awards).
[d]Average earnings in the three highest years of the last ten.
[e]Earnings above the maximum in one or more years.

Minimum Benefits Since its inception, the old-age pension program has had a minimum benefit. In the original legislation the guarantee was $10 per month. Over the years the minimum benefit has been periodically increased and in 1975 equaled $101.30 per month. In addition to this regular minimum for which all persons who achieve insured status are eligible, a special guarantee level was legislated in 1972 for long-term workers. Under the provisions of the special minimum, persons with 20 or more years in covered employment have a guaranteed level equal (in 1975) to $9 per month times the years of coverage in excess of 10 years (but not exceeding $180 per month).

Pechman, Aaron, and Taussig (1968) have succinctly summarized the major problem that arises when a minimum is provided:

> If minimum and low benefits were paid exclusively to aged householders with little or no other money income, the case for sharply increasing the minimum would be overwhelming. In the absence of an income test, however, many beneficiaries receive minimum or low benefits because they have had limited attachment to occupations covered by social security, not because they have had low lifetime earnings. Former employees of federal, state, and local governments can enter covered employment late in life and acquire insured status sufficient to entitle them to low or minimum benefits. . .

The recent introduction of a higher long term workers' minimum was, in part, a reaction to this problem. But the Advisory Council on Social Security felt that this action did not fully solve the problem and recommended in 1975 that the minimum benefit be frozen, resulting in a gradual decline in its real value in the years to come. This recommendation, however, has not been adopted by the Congress.

Dependent Benefits   As indicated above, a wife (and others) can receive a benefit based on her spouse's work experience and earnings. If a wife also works and becomes qualified for benefits based on her own work experience, she receives either the spouse benefit based on her husband's pension or a pension based upon her own work history, whichever is higher. Thus, the wife may pay social security taxes without adding to the family's retirement income.* The problem is further aggravated by the fact that the husband and wife are treated as separate taxable units and consequently may collectively pay more taxes than a family with only a single worker earning the same amount. This occurs as a result of the taxable-earnings ceiling that limits the taxed earnings of the single-earner family to the ceiling but taxes each earner of the dual-earner family up to the maximum.

As with the weighted benefit formula, the justification for the spouse benefit is made on social adequacy grounds: on a given earnings history, two people are less able (than one person) to provide *for* retirement and need more income *in* retirement. Pechman, Aaron, and Taussig (1968) argue, however, that the greater amount a couple gets (currently 50 percent more) is too large: "The benefits of single workers should be raised substantially, relative to those of married couples. A smaller increment than 50 percent is justified because, at any given earnings level, single persons now receive smaller benefits relative to their previous standard of living than do married couples."

Other critics of the spouse benefit argue that the improved real levels of current and future social security benefits (and improved levels of other retirement income) reduce the need for spouse benefits. Consideration, it is urged, should be given to eliminating this benefit or freezing the amounts at existing levels.

Still others have argued that a better way to recognize the retirement needs of spouses who do not enter the salaried labor force is to ex-

---

*If a husband and wife both work, the working wife has several advantages not available to the nonworking wife. She can retire and draw benefits at 62 or over even if her husband works on. Survivors' benefits—lump-sum, children's benefits, and parents' benefits—may be paid on her earnings record. Also, before age 65 she may draw disability benefits on her own record.

tend coverage and benefits to these nonsalaried household workers. West Germany recently added such a provision to its social security program.

Early Retirement   Up until 1956 workers could not receive their old-age pension until they reached the age of 65. The selection of age 65 for the receipt of benefits was a somewhat arbitrary decision of those who drafted the legislation. In large part the decision was simply to copy the age provisions of existing public and private pension programs, almost all of which used age 65.

In 1956 the social security law was changed to permit *women* workers to receive reduced benefits between the ages of 62–64; and in 1961 this option was extended to men. In both cases the reduction was to be the full actuarial amount. That is, persons receiving benefits before age 65 were to receive over their remaining lifetime amounts that—based on average life expectancy—would not exceed (on average) the total amounts received by those retiring at age 65.

From the very beginning, the early retirement option was exceedingly popular and has been exercised by large numbers of workers. The Social Security Administration reports that over half the men awarded initial retirement benefits each year since 1962 have received reduced benefits.

Delayed Retirement   In 1939 the calculation of the social security pension was changed to include a percent benefit increment for each year that credited earnings were at least $200. ''This provision thus gave an individual who postponed his retirement after 65 a larger benefit when he retired than if he began to draw his benefits at 65. This provision was the subject of much controversy and was repealed in the 1950 law so that higher current benefits could be paid without a cost increase.'' (Cohen, 1957)

In 1972 a provision was added to social security that raised benefits for those who delayed retirement beyond age 65. Subsequent to the provision canceled in 1950, persons who continued to work beyond age 64 totally lost their *potential* pension benefits available each year thereafter that they worked. The new provision reduces the loss somewhat but does not totally eliminate it. For there to be no loss in the actuarial value of a worker's benefit would require that his benefit level be increased by about 9 percent a year, instead of the 1 percent adjustment in the current law.

The Retirement Test   The retirement test reduces or eliminates social security benefit payments if an otherwise eligible recipient earns above an earnings exemption ceiling. Over the years officials of the Social Security Administration have acknowledged that this test generates the most questions and the most criticisms among people covered by the social security program. Further evidence of the controversy generated by this issue is the fact that in every session of Congress since 1940, numerous bills have been introduced to eliminate or liberalize the test.

The most recent Advisory Council on Social Security (1975) gives the following rationale for the test:

> The Council has reviewed the provisions of the retirement test and believes that the test is consistent with the basic purpose and principles of social security: to replace, in part, earnings lost because of retirement in old age, disability, or death. Complete elimination of the retirement test is inadvisable.
>
> The retirement test has been criticized because it does not take into account a beneficiary's income from such nonwork sources as dividends, rents, or pension payments. If the test took account of income other than earnings from work, it would no longer be a retirement test but an income test. If it became an income test, the fundamental idea that social security benefits are intended as a partial replacement of earnings from work would be diluted or lost.

While the reasoning advanced by the Advisory Council has also been the official position of the Social Security Administration, it is important to recognize two other arguments that are frequently made in support of the test:

First, since there are still many workers age 62 or older who do not receive social security benefits and since most of them are working full time, repeal of the retirement test would be relatively expensive and benefit most those who need help the least.

Second, given the fact that relatively high rates of unemployment have been a frequent phenomenon in the American economy, the retirement test encourages older workers to retire and thereby opens up job opportunities for younger workers. Moreover, older workers with pensions are discouraged from competing for jobs with younger workers by offering their services at wages below prevailing levels.

The work-disincentive result of the retirement test arises principally from the fact that, in effect, earnings above the maximum are "taxed" at the relatively high rate of 50 percent. Studies have shown that some older workers have a strong aversion to loss of benefits at this tax rate. The effect of the test, therefore, is to discourage some workers from staying in the labor force and also to set a limit on part-time work activity so that earnings do not go beyond the maximum.

While complete elimination of the retirement test would be costly and benefit many high earners, it can be argued alternatively that the test should be liberalized significantly to encourage and allow those people with low or moderate pension incomes to work in retirement. Various proposals have been advanced that would effectively exclude people with high earnings from the receipt of benefits but would not penalize low earners who wanted or needed to supplement their pension income. Complete *elimination* of the test is estimated by the Social Security Actuary to cost about $4 billion, but substantial *liberalization* could cost less than a billion.

The argument that older workers should retire to make room for younger workers raises a number of very complex issues. Ideally, an appropriate mix of monetary and fiscal policy by the government could promote an expansionary economy with jobs for almost everyone—thereby avoiding the dilemma of the older versus younger worker trade-off. The problem that arises, however, is that as the economy approaches full employment, inflationary factors tend to push up the general level of prices. Economic policy makers are thus faced with the unpleasant choice of trading off less employment to prevent more inflation.

In addition to having to choose between inflation and unemployment (sometimes referred to as the problem of "fine tuning" the economy) there is the problem of the recessions and depressions that have occurred throughout the century. The result of these has been millions of unemployed workers.

The causes of downturns in the economy are varied. While it is generally agreed that increased economic sophistication now provides nations with the necessary tools to prevent or moderate economic instability, the application of this knowledge has been far from perfect.

Given, then, the recurring instability and joblessness that have characterized the American economy, it is not surprising to find workers and unions supporting policies that promise to moderate the situation. Support of the retirement test appears to be one policy that falls into this category.

In contrast, the recent aging of the population is a factor that may undermine future worker support for the retirement test. As the costs to the working population of providing pensions to a growing segment of the total population significantly increase, there is apt to be better recognition of the fact that there is a relatively high price tag associated both with our present policies, which encourage or force people to retire, and with the alternative of abolishing the retirement test.

Survivors' Benefits   We are apt to forget that social security provides more than worker retirement pensions. Currently about 40 percent of the social security pensions being paid are to survivors and to disabled workers and their dependents—totaling about 12 million pensions in 1975.

When a worker protected by social security dies, a $255 lump-sum payment is made to the widow, widower, or (if neither) a person responsible for burial expenses. Qualifying widows, surviving divorced wives, children, and dependent parents are also paid monthly pensions. Conditions for receipt of a survivor's benefit vary considerably depending on the relation of the relative to the deceased.

Probably the two most important categories are widows (widowers) and children. A widow who was married to a fully insured worker for at least nine months, who is not married, and who has reached age 60 is entitled to a benefit of 100 percent of her husband's pension if payments begin at age 65 and a reduced benefit at an earlier age (71.5 percent at age 60). Benefits are in most cases reduced to 50 percent if the widow remarries, and subject to reduction if any earnings exceed the retirement test. Unmarried dependent children under age 18, disabled, or full-time students under 22 are entitled to a pension equal to 75 percent of the deceased parent's pension. A unanimous Supreme Court decision recently struck down a provision of the Social Security Act that prohibited widowers from receiving survivor benefits based on their wives' earnings.

Survivors' benefits are extremely important to the economic well-being of widows. A study by Lucy Mallan (1975) found, for example, that if social security were omitted from the total 1971 income of widows under age 60 with children, the proportion with poverty incomes would double, rising from one-third to almost 60 percent.

Social Security Pension Reform

Over the years there has been continuous complaining about the inadequacy of the pension levels, given the economic situation of the elderly. But in the early years the Congress did not respond to these complaints and to the generally acknowledged inadequate income situation of most elderly. Some people point to the legislated benefit increases occurring over the early years. But the fact is that except for the very early and the most recent years, these periodic increases did little more than keep benefit levels in line with the changing price level—which was also rising over time.

In recent years there has been mounting criticism of the old-age pension program with regard to two major issues: the adequacy of benefits (which has always been a major complaint) and alleged inequities existing among various recipient groups (which is a more recent development). These mounting criticisms have stimulated a renewed interest in both reform of social security and alternatives to it. The remainder of this chapter discusses the views of a number of groups and individuals who have studied the social security program and proposed various reforms.

The Social Security Advisory Council   The 1937–38 Advisory Council, authorized by the Senate Committee on Finance, was the first group of eminent persons asked to review the social security laws. Under current law, a new council is to be appointed every four years. Its function is to review all aspects of the social security program and to recommend improvements.

Over the years the various advisory councils have not called for any fundamental changes in the system. In general, the major efforts of these groups have been to concentrate on ways of *improving* the program through incremental changes. The modest efforts of past advisory councils result in part (a) because the council members are able to devote only limited time and get together relatively infrequently, and (b) because the councils have lacked their own permanent staff and have had to rely largely on suggestions and data provided by the Social Security Administration itself.

This does not mean that the advisory councils have not made important suggestions. The one in 1938–39 recommended, for example, survivors' benefits. The one in 1948–49 recommended expanded coverage, and the advisory council that met in 1970–71 recommended making the widow's benefit equal to 100 percent of the worker's benefit (as opposed to the 82½ percent under the then current law). These are examples of the kinds of suggestions the council makes. Such recommendations result in important improvements in the social security program but do not satisfy critics of the system, who charge that it is fundamentally inadequate and inequitable.

The large pension increase passed by Congress in 1972, which greatly exceeded rising cost-of-living needs, was a major effort to alleviate the inadequacy of social security benefits. It is interesting that the legislation was not stimulated by (or the result of) any recommendations of the Social Security Advisory Council or, for that matter, by recommendations of the various governmental task forces that had been appointed to review the problems of the elderly. Instead, early in his first term (1969) President Nixon sent a message to Congress proposing changes in social security. The key recommendations were, first, a 10 percent increase in benefits; second, and more importantly, a proposal that the Consumer Price Index be used to adjust automatically future benefits and that a wage index be used to adjust the contribution and benefit base.

At the same time that the President proposed changes in social security, he proposed a welfare reform bill—the Family Assistance Act. The House Ways and Means Committee and the Senate Finance Committee held hearings that simultaneously considered both the social security and welfare reforms. The major focus of these hearings, however, was on welfare reform and not on social security. Therefore, most of the testimony did not even mention the social security proposals.

At about the same time a new Social Security Advisory Council met and reported. This council had been appointed in the early part of the first Nixon Administration and the Administration had taken the position that aside from the changes recommended in its social security message, it would make no other legislative suggestions until the advisory council made its report. It argued that it would be premature for the Administration to make legislative proposals while this very illustrious group, which was given the job of surveying the whole situation, was still in the process of deliberating.

This position, of course, set up expectations that something significant would come out of the council's report. Nothing did. The council looked at a number of incremental changes, mostly equity changes, and rejected most of the proposals people had made. Instead, the 20 percent increase was first proposed by Senator Frank Church on the floor of the Senate and than supported by House Ways and Means Chairman, Wilbur Mills (at the time a presidential hopeful).

The only important recommendations coming out of the council's report were in the area of financing. The report argued strongly in favor of moving to a more pay-as-you-go system (changing from a "three-year reserve" to a "one-year reserve") and made a strong recommendation that the actuary use nonstatic assumptions when making projections of benefit outlays and contributions into the system—assume that earnings levels will rise over time, that the contribution and benefit base will increase as earnings rise, and that benefits will be increased as prices rise.

The most recent Advisory Council was appointed in 1974 and issued its report in 1975. The main focus of that report was again financing issues (discussed in Chapter 8). However, the council did make three benefit recommendations:

1. To reduce the retirement test "tax rate" from 50 percent to 33 1/3 percent between the exempt amount and twice the exempt amount (retaining the 50 percent rate above this interval).
2. To freeze the minimum benefit level.
3. To *stabilize* the earnings-replacement rates from social security at their 1975 levels by changing the automatic adjustment mechanism. (*See* p. 139, Chapter 8).

The 1971 White House Conference on Aging   The 1971 White House Conference on Aging was a highly structured event. One of the techniques used to develop social policy recommendations for the aged was: (a) to identify prior to the state and national conferences certain key issues, (b) to get those issues stated as succinctly as possible, and (c) to have backup material available for the delegates so that they could intelligently discuss the issues, make decisions, and formulate recommendations on each one. The conference planners attempted to develop procedures that would discourage the conference from making hundreds of relatively minor recommendations; what they sought were *a small number of very important recommendations.*

Conference delegates were split up into sections dealing with various areas of aging policy. Each section was faced with about four, but sometimes as high as ten, specified issues they had to discuss and react to before other proposals could be brought before the group. In the income section the first issue raised the question of what should be an adequate standard of living for the elderly. A separate issue dealt with how this income should be provided (i.e., what mix of public and private pension programs there should be).

Prior to the Washington conference each state had its own White House Conference. When faced with the choice between the Social Security Administration's poverty index as an income adequacy standard, the Bureau of Labor Statistics' older couple's budget, and a relative adequacy concept, most state conferences chose to endorse the BLS older couple's budget as a standard of adequate income. This recommendation was later reaffirmed at the national conference in Washington.

Apart from recommending this definition of "adequacy," the White House Conference delegates called for only two other major changes in social security old-age pensions: (a) partial funding of benefits out of general revenue, and (b) major liberalization of the retirement test.

Separating "Public Assistance" from Social Security
Switching from the public arena, let us now look at some recommendations that have been made by a group of economists at The Brookings Institution. Pechman, Aaron, and Taussig argue in their book

Social Security—Perspectives for Reform that the aged should be eligible for either an earnings-related pension or a negative income tax payment—whichever is the greater. They argue further that the earnings-related pension should have a replacement rate that is roughly the same at all earnings levels between subsistence and the level of median earnings. And they recommend that there be no spouse benefits but instead that pensions be based on total family earnings.

The major point Pechman, Aaron, and Taussig argue is that the social security system *should not operate both as a welfare system and a pension system*. If a person receives income in old age (including a social security pension) that places him in a taxable bracket, they feel that such a person should pay taxes (regardless of age). On the other hand, if the elderly person's income is too low, they argue that he should be eligible for a negative tax program:

> The advantage of the dual system is its efficiency and flexibility. Either part of the system could be altered independently of the other. At present any effort to improve social security with respect to the income support function typically requires substantial improvements with respect to the earnings replacement function. For example, a program to raise minimum benefits to help the aged poor must in practice be joined with a general benefit increase, thereby making the cost of aiding the poor seem greater than it is. This is aggravated, of course, by the fact that the present system supplements income regardless of the income status of the beneficiaries. In many instances higher minimum benefits would be paid to individuals with adequate income. Under the proposed system the earnings related benefit could be set at any desired percentage of past earnings. Negative income tax allowances to those with low earnings histories would be sufficient to keep income above poverty level. Thus, policy makers and the public could identify immediately the cost of performing the two distinct functions of the system. (Pechman, Aaron, Taussig, 1968)

The advantage Pechman, Aaron and Taussig (and various other economists) see in separating the two issues is seen as a disadvantage by others. Some writers in the field of income-maintenance policy argue that when you separate the two groups (and hence make it very clear whom you're helping), it is very difficult to get sufficient political support for improving the situation of the poor. They argue that the only way one can get help for the poor is to piggyback it onto help for middle- (and even upper-) income groups. For example, one authority on social security, Wilbur Cohen, has argued that "in the United States, a program that deals only with the poor will end up being a poor program. There is every evidence that this is true. Ever since the Elizabethan Poor Law of 1601, programs only for the poor have been lousy, no good, *poor* programs. And a program that is only for the poor—one that has nothing in it for the middle income and the upper income—is, in the long run, a program the American public won't support. This is why I think we must try to find a way to link the interests of all classes in these programs." (Cohen and Friedman, 1972)

Changing the Pension Adequacy Standard In recent years there has been less talk about eliminating poverty among the elderly and, instead, more attention given to providing them with "adequate income." Many people have begun to argue that benefits should be related to some kind of retirement budget based on observed needs and lifestyles of the elderly. The 1971 White House Conference on Aging, for example, recommended that adequate income be defined by the Bureau of Labor Statistics' budget for an elderly couple.

The Bureau of Labor Statistics' budgets are for retired couples who are "self-supporting, living independently in their own home, in reasonably good health, and able to take care of themselves." The generalized conception of the living standard is translated into a list of commodities and services that can be priced. The "intermediate level" budget is currently around $6000 per year for an elderly couple.

The establishment of such a budget standard (or even a variety of budgets) for various groups or categories of the aged can never (and is not intended to) adequately reflect the even greater variety of economic circumstances of these aged families prior to retirement. The budgets do "not show how an 'average' retired couple actually spends its money, nor does it show how a couple should spend its money. . . . In general, however, the representative list of goods and services comprising the standard reflects the collective judgment of families as to what is necessary and desirable. . . ." (U.S. Bureau of Labor Statistics, 1966). Thus, the Nixon Administration responded to the adequacy of income recommendations of the 1971 White House Conference delegates as follows:

> The Administration does not concur in the recommendations of the delegates to the Conference that the "intermediate" budget developed by the Bureau of Labor Statistics become the national goal in this area. . . . While these [budget] studies are interesting and useful in their own right, they provide no basis for knowing whether any particular level of income is "adequate" under varying sets of circumstances.

Also, while it is easy to adjust these budgets for price changes, it is much more difficult to adjust them so that they reflect the changing levels of living in the economy; such adjustments contain a high degree of arbitrariness.

An alternative way (other than poverty indexes or budget levels) of specifying for policy purposes the operational income-maintenance goals of various pension programs is to specify the proportion of prior earnings that are to be guaranteed to the worker upon retirement through a pension program(s). In recent years the pension systems of many countries have sought to express pension benefits as a proportion of earnings.

But in the United States, aside from general recommendations calling for helping the aged by improving social security (which often take the form of requesting 5, 10, 20, or 50 percent benefit increases), there has been very little discussion of just what the level of old-age benefits should be.

Over the years the principal architect of United States social security reform has been the House Committee on Ways and Means of the Congress. In 1967 that committee issued a report that discussed the earnings-replacement objective that was used to explain the benefit levels specified in the social security amendments of 1967. The report said, in part:

> The bill embodies the principle that the retirement benefit of a man age 65 and his wife should represent at least 50 percent of his average wages under the social security system. . . . In establishing the benefit levels, it was necessary for your committee to consider not only benefit levels but also earnings levels and other factors. It was the committee's judgment that when all factors were taken in conjunction, the benefit for a couple which is based on the maximum credited earnings ought to be approximately 50 percent of the average earnings of the worker, with an appropriate increase in the percentage as the earnings fell below the maximum, until benefits reached what in the light of existing conditions seemed to be an appropriate minimum benefit. (U.S. Committee on Ways and Means, 1967)

A pension formula that seeks to replace 50 percent of *lifetime* average earnings, however, usually replaces a much lower percentage of earnings *just prior to retirement*. The actual social security pension replacement rates for American couples retiring, for example, between 1960 and 1980 (estimated by a simulation model) tend to be much lower than the committee's goal. If pensions are compared with the average of earnings five years prior to retirement, one finds that a majority of the couples will receive at least 50 percent replacement only in the earnings groups below $4000. In general, couples will receive much lower than 50 percent replacement. (Schulz, et al., 1974)

Schulz, et al. argue in *Providing Adequate Income in Retirement* that a pension program that replaces such a low proportion of prior earnings is not an adequate floor of protection and that the House Ways and Means Committee's 50 percent standard is inadequate *as long as it is based upon unadjusted lifetime earnings.* Pensions based on a lifetime earnings average, by the very nature of the averaging process, are reflective of a living standard experienced decades before retirement. One would expect families to have become accustomed to the higher living standard typically associated with the later years before retirement and would not expect the act of retirement to change dramatically their living expectations.

Another major defect of the lifetime earnings measure proposed by the Ways and Means Committee is that it does not take inflation into account. Over the lifetime of any individual it is certain that some significant amount of inflation will occur. Failure to adjust past earnings for subsequent inflation gives a distorted and unmeaningful measure.

Thus, it is certainly not unreasonable to base individual and collective retirement pension plans on a goal of preventing any major decline in lifestyle as a result of retirement. In fact, the "golden years" of retirement are often glamorized as those years when an individual is finally free of work constraints and able to enjoy life more.

In their book, Schulz, et al. report on innovative pension reform that has taken place in four countries. In three of these countries—Germany, Sweden, and Belgium—the objective of "maintaining living standards during retirement" was an important consideration in designing the current pension program. The authors believe that this is the direction the United States should take in reform of pensions. They argue that the United States should formulate new policies to improve both private and public pensions—starting not with a *poverty* standard of adequacy but rather using a standard that recognizes the desirability and reasonableness of maintaining past living standards in retirement. Specifically, they propose "the adoption of an adequacy of income standard for social security old-age benefits which would provide inflation protected benefits equal to at least 55 percent of the individual's or family's (if married) *preretirement* average earnings during the best ten of the last fifteen years prior to retirement (with specified minimum and maximum benefit levels)" (pp. 270–271).

It would be possible to modify the current social security old-age pension program in the United States along the lines suggested above, and still maintain many of the founding principles of social security discussed previously. The old-age pension program in the United States was designed as an insurance program for the replacement of earnings loss due to retirement, has always related benefits to prior earnings, and implicitly specifies a rate of earnings replacement through its benefit calculation formula.

But the new proposed adequacy standard does represent a substantial movement away from a view of social security as a minimal floor of protection. To implement the new adequacy standard requires (a) a more widespread recognition of the earnings-replacement implications of the program, (b) a more detailed study of the replacement rates achieved by the present regulations of the program, and—most importantly—(c) a collective decision regarding changes required to improve the earnings-replacement potential of the program for all or various categories of beneficiaries.

Schulz argues that the establishment of more adequate collective public pensions based upon this standard need not discourage individual initiative nor eliminate private pensions. Instead, it would give individuals a more secure base upon which to base their personal saving decisions and encourage private pensions to expand and more adequately deal with the "special problems," unique needs, or varying retirement preferences of different groups of workers.

Other Social Security Programs

In previous chapters we have made reference to a number of programs other than retirement pension programs that have an important impact on the economic welfare of the aged. It is appropriate at this point to present additional information on some of them, since they are all important complements to retirement pension programs.*

Disability Disability protection under social security is currently provided to: (a) disabled insured workers and their dependents, (b) disabled widows and widowers of insured workers, and (c) the adult (18 or older) sons and daughters of insured disabled, retired, or deceased workers who become disabled before age 22. Disability protection was not legislated until 1956. While it had been proposed repeatedly, major groups opposed it, and early social security advisory groups disagreed about the predictability of disability program costs and about whether one could administratively determine eligibility for this type of benefit (i.e., distinguish legitimate disability from malingering).

When the first major legislative proposals for disability protection were debated in 1949 and 1950, strong criticism and opposition were voiced by the American Medical Association, the United States Chamber of Commerce, the National Manufacturers Association, and representa-

*Not discussed are the food stamp program and veterans' benefits.

tives of private insurance organizations. After the defeat of the 1949–50 bill, strong opposition continued in succeeding years to the various new proposals that were introduced—including the disability freeze amendment of 1954* and the social security disability benefits finally legislated in 1956. All the disability proposals were attacked as potentially costly, difficult to administer, and the beginning of "socialized medicine." Given this strong opposition over the years, the ultimate passage of disability legislation in 1956 is viewed by many as a major development in the legislative history of social security in the United States.

To be eligible for social security disability payments a worker must be screened on three levels: (a) determination of insured status, (b) assessment of physical condition and level of functional impairment, and (c) determination of ability to work. To achieve insured status, the worker must have 1 quarter of work coverage credit for each year since 1950 (or since age 21, if later) and 20 quarters of coverage during the 50-quarter period prior to disability. Disability, for purposes of benefit entitlement, is defined as "inability to engage in any substantial gainful activity by reason of any medically determinable physical or mental impairment which can be expected to result in death or which has lasted or can be expected to last for a continuous period of not less than 12 months."

The disability pension is based on average earnings (excluding the disablement period) and is calculated in the same way as old-age pensions, using the same formula and the same minimum benefit level. Initially the social security disability benefit was reduced dollar-for-dollar by any workmen's compensation benefits received by the same worker. Then in 1958 this deduction was removed, and considerable controversy followed. Turnbull, Williams, and Cheit (1967) report that criticism arose over the fact that with the deduction removed, "it became possible in some states for a seriously injured worker to receive combined benefits that would exceed his wages prior to his disability." Faced with the criticisms of those who feared the encroachment and possible supplantation of federal disability insurance for state and private programs, Congress reintroduced an offset provision in 1965. Under the new provision, social security disability and workmen's compensation payments together could not exceed 80 percent of a high-5-year average of earnings in covered employment (adjusted periodically for rises in wage levels). Then in 1972 the definition of average earnings was changed to permit benefits to be based (if a higher benefit resulted) on average

---

*A provision that prevented periods of disability from reducing or wiping out retirement and survivors' benefits by "freezing" the individual's rights at the time of disablement. For a good discussion of the legislative history of this and other disability provisions, see Cohen (1957), Chapter 4.

monthly earnings in the calendar year of *highest* earnings during the 5 years preceding the year in which disability began.

Thus, as the disability benefit has evolved, the disabled worker is guaranteed the social security minimum pension and up to 80 percent earnings replacement (in cases of dual eligibility for social security and workmen's compensation).

In fact, there are not two but three major public disability programs: the federal social security disability program, the federal Supplemental Security Income program, which provides benefits to low-income disabled, aged, and blind persons, and the workmen's compensation programs (administered by state governments), which provide insurance against industrial accident and occupational disease. In addition, about two-thirds of private wage and salary workers have some kind of protection against loss of earnings caused by *short-term, nonoccupational* disability. Most of this protection comes from private group disability insurance or formal paid sick-leave plans. Five states (and Puerto Rico), however, have established state plans, which currently cover about 15 million workers.

The existence of multiple and overlapping public and private disability programs has resulted in a continuing debate over the adequacy and equity of the resulting nonsystem. Merton Bernstein (1973), for example, has charged that the ensuing "web of protection provided by separate public and private programs is full of holes, with those most in need receiving less protection than those with lesser need." As we indicate in Chapter 9, the problems of workers unable to continue working until the normal retirement age because of disability and other causes represents one of the policy areas requiring major attention in the years to come.

In recent years there has been a dramatic increase in the number of disability awards under social security and projected deficits in the disability trust fund. Under repeated questioning by Congress, the Social Security Administration has been unable to offer a satisfactory explanation of this apparently growing problem. (*See*, for example, Cardwell, 1975)

Medicare In 1965 the Social Security Act was amended to establish two related health insurance plans covering virtually all persons aged 65 and over and certain severely disabled persons under age 65 (by an amendment in 1972). Persons eligible for any type of social security or railroad retirement monthly benefit are automatically eligible; legislation passed in 1972 provides voluntary enrollment for persons who do not automatically qualify but who pay the full cost of the insurance coverage.

Basic protection, financed through compulsory contributions paid while working, provides partial payment of the costs of inpatient hospital services and certain posthospital extended care. Supplemental medical benefits are available on a voluntary basis to people paying a monthly premium. After a participant has paid an initial deductible amount, this supplemental plan pays 80 percent of the "reasonable charges" or costs for physician and surgeon services (regardless of where furnished), certain outpatient hospital services, outpatient physical therapy, limited ambulance services, and a variety of miscellaneous expenses.

Medicaid An amendment of the Social Security Act in 1950 provided for federal financial participation in providing medical care to public assistance recipients, and in 1960 another amendment authorized additional federal matching for medical-care payments for Old-Age Assistance recipients. Then in 1965 the Medicaid program was enacted as Title XIX of the Social Security Act.

Medicaid provides federal funds appropriated from general revenue to states establishing qualifying medical assistance programs. All states except Arizona participate. The federal cost-sharing ranges from 50 percent to 80 percent based on a formula that varies the percentage in accordance with a state's per capita income.

A wide measure of discretion is allowed states under the Medicaid legislation with regard to what groups (aged and nonaged) are eligible for benefits and what income and asset "means tests" will be applied to various individuals. Consequently, actual practice among the states varies greatly. In 1970, 39 percent of Medicaid dollars were spent to provide medical care for persons age 65 or older. (U.S. Joint Economic Committee, 1972)

Participating states are required to provide both inpatient and outpatient hospital services, skilled nursing home or home health care services, and physicians' services. Other services, such as drugs, dental services, and physical therapy, are provided at the option of the state.

The Supplemental Security Income Program A new cash-assistance program for the needy aged, blind, and disabled went into operation at the beginning of 1974. This Supplemental Security Income program (SSI) replaced federal grants to the three programs: the state-administered programs of old-age assistance (OAA), aid to the blind (AB), and aid to the permanently and totally disabled (APTD). The SSI program is financed from general revenues of the federal government and establishes uniform eligibility requirements and benefits levels for the whole nation. In addition, states are encouraged (and some are re-quired) to supplement the federal benefits with their own payments.

Eligibility for this program requires meeting an asset test, and benefits are phased out as income increases. Nonexcluded assets may not exceed $1500 for an individual and $2250 for a couple. Excluded assets are (a) the value of a home up to $25,000 (fair market value), (b) nonliquid-income-producing property, (c) assets of a blind or disabled person needed to establish a "self-support plan," (d) the value of house-hold goods and personal effects up to $1500, an automobile (up to $1200), and life insurance (cash surrender value up to $1500), (e) self-support business property, and (f) cash reimbursement from qualifying indemnity insurance.

Benefits are reduced by 100 percent of all *unearned* income and 50 percent of *earned* income amounts above the "disregard." The two major income disregards are $60 per quarter of irregular unearned in-come and the first $85 per month of earned income.

The benefit paid to eligible individuals is $1892 per year (1975) and $2839 for couples. This benefit is about three-quarters of the non-farm poverty level for aged individuals and about 90 percent for a couple. The federal benefit is automatically increased for changes in the cost of living.

When SSI was legislated, its supporters argued that it would re-duce many of the traditional problems associated with other programs to help the poor—more efficient program administration, less stigma to recipients, and more adequate benefits using a national standard. During the first years of the program the Social Security Administration had difficulty coping with the new responsibilities and workload suddenly thrust upon it as the chief administrator of the new program. After these transitional problems are solved, we will get a better idea of just how successful the program has been and its potential for the future.

Suggested Readings

Booth, Philip. *Social Security in America.* Ann Arbor: Institute of Labor and Industrial Relations, University of Michigan and Wayne State, 1973.
    A good survey of all the OASDHI programs and a discussion of many of the problems, as the author sees them.
Cohen, Wilbur, J., and Milton Friedman. *Social Security: Universal or Selective?* Rational Debate Seminars. Washington, D.C.: The American Enterprise Institute, 1972.
    A debate between former HEW Secretary Cohen, who defends social security, and economist Friedman, who argues for its abolition.

International Labour Office. *An Introduction to Social Security*. Geneva: ILO, 1970.
> Developed for use throughout the world, this comprehensive discussion stresses the basic principles and alternatives for social security systems. Conceptual issues and practical problems are given extensive examination.

Lubove, Roy. *The Struggle for Social Security, 1900–1935*. Cambridge, Mass.: Harvard University Press, 1968.
> An interpretive, historical analysis of the passage of the 1935 Social Security Act.

Pechman, Joseph A.; Henry J. Aaron; and Michael K. Taussig. *Social Security—Perspectives for Reform*. Washington, D.C.: The Brookings Institution, 1968.
> Despite its age (which means that program descriptions are not up to date), this book remains one of the best discussions of the issues associated with old-age pensions under social security.

Rimlinger, Gaston. *Welfare Policy and Industrialization in Europe, America, and Russia*. New York: Wiley, 1971.
> A comparative analysis of the historical development of the social security systems in Germany, Russia, Great Britain, and the United States.

Schulz, James; Guy Carrin; Hans Krupp; Manfred Peschke; Elliott Sclar; and J. Van Steenberge. *Providing Adequate Retirement Income—Pension Reform in the United States and Abroad*. Hanover, N.H.: New England Press for Brandeis University Press, 1974.
> This book gives major attention to concepts of pension adequacy and analyzes practices in various countries with innovative social security pension programs.

U.S. Social Security Administration. *Social Security Programs in the United States*. Washington, D.C.: U.S. Government Printing Office, various years.
> Describes the provisions of the OASDHI, unemployment insurance, workmen's compensation, temporary disability, and public-assistance programs in the United States. It is revised periodically so readers should make sure they have the most recent issue.

Wilson, Thomas, ed. *Pensions, Inflation and Growth*. London: Heinemann Educational Books, 1974.
> Studies of pensions in the Federal Republic of Germany, the Netherlands, Sweden, Italy, France, Belgium. Emphasis is given to the methods used by various countries to adjust pensions for inflation and growth.

Chapter Seven

What Role for
Private Pensions?

Pension plans set up by private industry or employee groups did not appear in the United States until the end of the nineteenth century.The first company pension plan was established by the American Express Company in 1875 but provided benefits only to *permanently incapacitated* workers over age 60 who had at least 20 years of service.Thereafter plans were established in the railroad industry and by a few firms in other industries. However, a congressional study reports that such pension schemes "were by and large slow in developing and [that] there were probably fewer than ten plans in operation by the end of the 19th century." (U.S. House Committee on Educational Labor, 1972)

The Civil Service Retirement Act was enacted in 1920, providing pension coverage for the first time to federal civilian employees. A year later the implementation of private plans was encouraged by the Revenue Act of 1921; this legislation exempted from income taxation both the *income* of pension and profit-sharing trusts and the *employer contributions* to these plans.

Although between 3 and 4 million workers were covered by private pensions prior to the establishment of social security, coverage was concentrated in only a few industries; benefits were very limited; less than 15 percent of the work force was covered; and payments were made only if certain very stringent age and service requirements were met. It was not until the 1940's and 1950's that the growth of private pensions mushroomed. Coverage rose from about 4 million employees in the late thirties to roughly 10 million in 1950 to 20 million in 1960.

Various factors have been cited as responsible for this rather dramatic increase in private pension coverage:

1. Continued industrialization of the American economy, together with a movement of workers out of agriculture, which stimulated increasing interest in alternatives other than the family for providing retirement security.
2. The introduction of private pensions by some employers as a way of creating employee loyalty and discouraging job shifting, since most early plans called for the worker to lose his rights to the pension if he left the firm.
3. Wage freezes during World War II and the Korean war that encouraged fringe-benefit growth in lieu of wages.
4. A series of favorable tax inducements offered by the federal government beginning with the Revenue Acts of 1921 and 1926. Probably the most important inducement was offered in the Revenue Act of 1942. Coming at a time of sharp federal personal and corporate income tax increases, the 1942 act: (a) treated employer contributions to qualified pension plans as tax deductible, (b) excluded plan-investment income from taxation, and (c) deferred taxes on participant beneficiaries until actually received in retirement.
5. A favorable decision by the Supreme Court in 1949 supporting the National Labor Relations Board's decision that pensions were a proper issue for collective bargaining.
6. The report of the Steel Industry Fact-Finding Committee in 1949, which included a recommendation that the industry had a social obligation to provide workers with pensions.
7. Growing recognition by unions of the inadequacy of social security benefits and the need for supplementation.
8. The development of multi-employer pension plans—particularly in the construction, transportation, trade, and service industries.

Currently there are over 30 million wage and salary workers in private industry covered by pension and deferred profit-sharing plans sponsored unilaterally or jointly by employers and/or employees. In addition, there are government employee plans covering approximately 15 million workers.

Retired workers receiving private pensions are in the minority. The Social Security Administration estimates that in 1973 a little over 6 million persons received private pension benefits. These beneficiaries were paid a total of $11.2 billion, which averages out to less than $2000 per beneficiary. Of course, the per capita figure does not give us a picture of how these benefits were actually distributed among the various recipients. While data are not available for 1973, an earlier survey provides this type of information. Figure 9 shows that while about half of the men receiving private pensions had annual benefits of 1 to 3 thousand dollars, 20 percent received less than $1000 and 32 percent received over $3000 (9 percent over $5000).

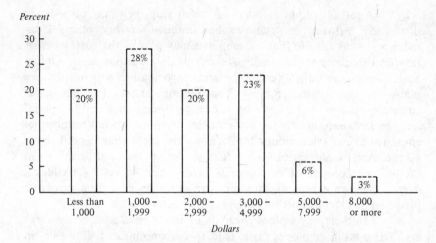

Figure 9. Private Pension Recipients: Distribution of Benefits from Longest Job, Men Retiring June 1969-June 1970[a]

Source: Walter W. Kolodrubetz, "Private Retirement Benefits and Relationship to Earnings: Survey of New Beneficiaries," *Social Security Bulletin* (May 1973): 16–37.
[a]The survey was restricted to persons also entitled to social security benefits.

Private Plan Characteristics

It is difficult to generalize about the provisions of private pension plans because of the large number of different plans with widely varying characteristics. There are about a half-million corporate pension plans in the United States. These can be generally divided into *single-employer* and *multi-employer* plans. Multi-employer plans usually require employers to make contributions into a central fund (typically a specified percent of payroll or cents-per-hour-worked), and employees can qualify for benefits from the fund by meeting eligibility requirements through employment in the various firms participating in the program. Reciprocity agreements among some of these multi-employer plans (and a few single-employer plans) allow workers to move between plans. Another important difference between the two types of plans is in their administration. Single-employer plans are generally managed by the employer alone; multi-employer plans are almost invariably administered by a group of trustees, with equal representation from labor and management (in accordance with terms of the Taft-Hartley Act).

Another common way of classifying private plans is to distinguish between *contributory* and *noncontributory* plans. Contributory plans require that the employee pay part of the cost, whereas noncontributory plans are financed solely by the employer. In the United States, most covered workers (80 percent) participate in noncontributory plans—in part because employ*er* contributions are tax free but under current federal laws employ*ee* contributions (unless sheltered by special arrangements) are not. Also, noncontributory plans do not require the employer to put aside money for *each* worker at the time benefit rights accrue. And employers can use actuarial assumptions that permit them (a) to take account of employee turnover prior to vesting (reducing current pension expenses), and (b) to raise the level of funding of the plan over an extended period of time (see Chapter 8).

Multi-employer plans cover about one-third of all covered workers. These multi-employer plans tend to be concentrated, however, in particular industries (mining, construction, trade, transportation, and service) and, in these industries, affect more than 50 percent of all covered workers.

In surveying the specific provisions of various pension plans, there are four key characteristics that are generally considered most important: the benefit formulas, vesting and portability requirements, the availability of survivors' benefits, and early retirement options.

Benefit Determination   While there is a great deal of variation among private plans in the way benefits are calculated, eight major types can be identified:

Defined Benefit Plans:

1. *Flat benefits*—the same benefit is provided all eligible retirees, usually either a flat dollar amount or the same specified percentage of past compensation.
2. *Service-only formulas*—benefits are proportionate to the number of years of credited employment.
3. *Earnings-only formulas*—benefits are based upon the employee's earnings over specified periods of employment (e.g., career, highest, terminal, or "last years" of earning).
4. *Combined service/earnings formulas*—benefits are based on both years of service and earnings.
5. *Social security offset formulas*—benefits are calculated by deducting all or part of an employee's social security benefit from the amount computed according to the private pension plan formula.
6. *Social security step-rate formulas*—benefits are calculated by a formula that provides higher benefits above a specified amount—usually the maximum earnings used to compute social security benefits at the time the formula was adopted or amended.

Defined Contribution Plans:

7. *Money-purchase arrangements*—periodic contributions are set aside according to a predetermined, or agreed upon, formula (usually a percent of earnings). Pensions are paid out based on the accumulated funds (contributions plus investment income) in individual employee accounts.
8. *Deferred profit-sharing plans*—contributions and benefits under these plans are not known in advance. Instead they depend on the profits of the employer and specified sharing-formulas.

The overwhelming proportion of workers covered *under single-employer plans* are covered by plans that use one of the formula types basing benefits (all or in part) on earnings. In contrast, only a small proportion of workers *under multi-employer plans* participate in plans using earnings-based formulas. Instead, most multi-employer plans either provide a flat benefit or use a service-only formula. Money-purchase plans are most common in public employee retirement systems and nonprofit organizations.

The most important trend in recent years has been a shift to basing benefits on earnings just prior to retirement. The major advantage of this type of formula is that it has a built-in adjustment for inflation *prior to retirement*—since earnings over time are usually adjusted upward for increases in the cost of living. All these formulas better reflect an employee's standard of living at retirement.

Vesting and Portability Requirements   Vesting and portability are related pension concepts but are not identical. Vesting refers to the provision in pension plans that guarantees that those covered by the plan will receive all or part of the benefit that they have earned (i.e., has accrued), whether or not they are working under the plan at the time of their retirement. Through vesting, the pension rights of otherwise qualified workers are protected whether they are discharged, furloughed, or quit voluntarily. Prior to the 1974 pension reform law (which established a variety of controls over private pensions), vesting provisions were often nonexistent. Where vesting was available, eligibility conditions varied greatly, and many workers lost their pension rights—sometimes after long years of service and sometimes just prior to retirement. The 1974 law now requires all plans covered by the law to provide minimum vested benefits meeting one of three alternative standards:

1. Vesting of 100 percent of accrued benefits after 10 years of service.
2. Vesting of 25 percent of accrued benefits after 5 years of service,

going up by 5 percent each year for the next 5 years and by 10 percent thereafter (until 100 percent vesting is reached after 15 years).
3. Vesting of 50 percent of accrued benefits when age and service add up to 45 years, with 100 percent vesting 5 years thereafter—subject to a minimum 5 years service and the constraint that employees must be 50 percent vested after 10 years of service and 100 percent vested after 15 years.

One problem that arises with vesting is that vested benefits left in a pension plan after a worker voluntarily or involuntarily leaves the firm are not adjusted upward if the pension plan's formula for *continuing* workers is changed either to compensate for inflation or to provide a higher level of real benefits.* "Portability" of pension rights permits employees to transfer the money value of these rights into another plan and, hopefully, by this process to reduce the inflationary losses that arise when benefits are left behind. Unfortunately, although portability has received a lot of public attention (and is often confused with vesting), the administrative, financial, and actuarial complexities of setting up such arrangements have discouraged any significant action in this area. One type of pension plan, the multi-employer plan, reduces the problems associated with job change by introducing limited portability (i.e., within the boundaries of the plan) through a *centralized* pension fund.

The 1974 pension reform law permits a separated employee to transfer *tax free* the value of a vested benefit into an "individual retirement account" *if permitted by the plan* or to another plan *if permitted by both plans.* In fact, an employer with a noncontributory plan has a positive financial incentive not to agree to this transfer, since he can earn interest or dividends on any "funded" money he keeps and need not pass on any of these earnings to the former employee.

Survivors' Benefits Half of the aged who are poor are widowed women. Provisions for survivors in pension plans, both public and private, play an important role in determining that outcome. For example, in a study of members of the United Auto Workers (UAW) and their survivors, Eugene Loren and Thomas Barker (1968) found that total resources available to survivors were inadequate for long-term needs. *More importantly, they found that without group survivors' benefits, vast numbers of survivors would be virtually destitute.* About 65 percent of the surveyed UAW families had financial resources at the worker's death of less than $3000; approximately half of the dependent surviving units had little or no net assets to supplement survivors' benefits or work income.

*Also, vested benefits left in plans with earnings-related formulas do not reflect the rise in earnings that would occur if the worker remained employed by the firm.

Detailed data on the operation of group plans other than for UAW employees are sparse; the general information that does exist clearly suggests that private pension plans until very recently have been contributing very little to the income maintenance of persons who survive after a worker's death.* In most private plans the worker has had to bear personally the *entire* burden of protecting his spouse through a "joint and survivor's option." Under this option a worker has to *elect* a reduction in his pension to cover the actuarial cost of a survivor's benefit for his spouse. Evidence indicates that few workers in the past, when faced with this choice, exercised the survivor's option. Relatively few plans *automatically* provided benefits to survivors after the death of the *active* worker, or, in fewer cases, the retired worker.

A 1968 Bureau of Labor Statistics survey of "100 selected pension plans under collective bargaining" provided information on the different pension approaches of firms to the problem of survivors. In 1968:

1. The most common kind of death benefit was a monthly payment to the survivor, paid only for a period of 6 months to 5 years.
2. Another common benefit was one that appeared in plans where the employee had made previous contributions to the plan. The benefit merely returned the employee's contribution to the survivor(s), together with the interest accrued on it.
3. The next most common type of benefit was a lump-sum payment. Here the most frequently paid amount by firms using this device was less than $5000.
4. The least common type of death benefit was one that gave the survivor(s) a benefit that was some percentage of the normal retirement benefit of the retiree.

A more recent survey by the Bureau of Labor Statistics (Hodgens, 1973) indicates that changes in survivors' benefit provisions have been occurring. In large part because of collective bargaining efforts by a few of the biggest unions, there has been a significant increase in the number of workers *automatically* covered by survivors' benefits. A sample survey of all private pension plans covering 26 or more participants in 1971 found 176 out of 1457 plans (12 percent) with automatic survivors' benefits covering about 20 percent of all plan participants. (Hodgens, 1973) About 99 percent of the covered workers were in plans that provided protection to the survivors of workers who died while employed. But about 35 percent of these workers were in plans that *eliminated* the survivors' benefits once the worker retired!

*Employers often provide group life insurance, and a few provide group survivor income benefits.

Because most of the plans aimed at protecting survivors of long-term employees, 4 out of 5 workers had to satisfy a minimum age and service requirement before survivors' benefits were payable. The most common requirements were being at least 55 years of age and having 10–15 years of service.

With regard to benefit amounts, the 1971 Bureau of Labor Statistics' survey found that benefits based on automatic provisions ranged from 30 to 100 percent of the worker's accrued pension benefit. About 40 percent of the workers were in plans paying 50 percent of the worker's pension; 27 percent were in plans paying 51 to 54 percent.

The Employee Retirement Income Security Act of 1974 (ERISA) requires that all annuity-paying retirement plans subject to the law must now provide a joint and survivor annuity to workers retiring at the normal retirement age *unless the employee elects otherwise.* Individual plans, however, are permitted under the law to establish their own rules that may deny employees the option of rejecting a survivors' benefit. But the law does not require the pension plan to "subsidize" the joint and survivor feature (although the plan is permitted to do so).

Given the large number of early retirees, it is important to note that the 1974 law operates in a reverse manner for those eligible to retire prior to the normal retirement age. For early retirees, the joint and survivor provisions need not be applicable under the plan *unless the employee makes an affirmative election.*

Early Retirement Options   Early retirement options in private pension plans permit workers to leave unemployment and receive benefits before the normal retirement age specified in the plan. Receipt of pension benefits at an earlier age almost always requires that the worker meet a minimum age requirement, a years-of-service requirement, or both. Many plans permit early retirement only with the employer's consent, and a few plans permit the employer to involuntarily retire the worker at an early age. The most common service requirement for early retirement is 10–15 years.

In 1969, almost 90 percent of all workers covered by private pension plans were in plans having early retirement options. In almost every plan up until the 1970's a worker exercising the early retirement option had his or her benefit reduced, usually by (or close to) the appropriate actuarial reduction. In recent years, however, a number of plans have begun providing a benefit that is greater than the actuarial equivalent.

One special type of early retirement option gives the worker a bigger benefit before social security benefits begin and then reduces the private pension benefit when social security begins. The benefit structure is usually constructed so that the worker receives a uniform benefit throughout his retirement—initially from the private pension alone and then from his combined pensions.

A study of 149 major pension plans by the Bureau of Labor Statistics (Hodgens, 1975) found that 40 percent of the plans had liberalized one or more aspects of their early retirement benefit provisions between the summer of 1970 and the fall of 1974. About one-third of the plans liberalized age and service requirements by lowering them or creating more flexibility. Moreover, during the 4-year period, 24 plans made normal retirement possible before age 65.

Private Pension Legislation

While the benefit formulas, vesting, survivors' provisions, and early retirement options are four of the most important aspects of private pensions, there are still others that have great significance for evaluating private pensions and determining public policy toward them. One of these areas concerns the danger of lost pension rights as a result of inadequate pension funding, misuse of pension funds, or the termination of plans because of plant closures, bankruptcy, or other reasons.

A great deal of attention has been given to this area by investigating groups and legislative committees. Congressional concern for the protection of employee benefit funds caused the enactment of the Welfare and Pension Plan Disclosure Act in 1959 but placed primary responsibility for policing the plans on the participants themselves. The Employee Retirement Income Security Act of 1974 set up a more comprehensive set of safeguards—establishing participation, vesting, and funding standards, plan-termination insurance, and extensive reporting and disclosure requirements. The major provisions of the act are:

1. Plans must minimally vest benefits using one of three alternatives (see pages 117–118).
2. Plan-termination insurance is established, up to $750 monthly, for employees whose plans terminate with insufficient funds.
3. Funding standards are established and fiduciary standards are strengthened.
4. Individual retirement accounts (exempt from federal income taxation) may be established by workers without private or public employee pension coverage, up to $1500 annually or 15 percent of annual compensation (whichever is less) may be invested.

5. New disclosure regulations permit participants to request once each year a statement from the plan administrator of total benefits, both vested and nonvested, that have accrued and the earliest date on which unvested benefits will become nonforfeitable.
6. The Social Security Administration receives reports from employers (through the Treasury Department) of vested benefits due separated workers; Social Security notifies employees of all vested pension rights at the time they apply for social security benefits.
7. With the consent and cooperation of their employers, employees may transfer upon separation vested pension rights on a tax free basis from one employer to another; or the employee may transfer the funds to an "individual retirement account."

Passed by both houses of Congress by wide vote margins, the new law (as its name implies) is an attempt to provide greater certainty that private pension promises will be fulfilled. But the legislation does not deal with all the problem areas that have been discussed in connection with private pensions. Critics have been quick to cite the problems they think still remain:

1. A large segment (over half) of the private work force still remains uncovered.
2. Very few private pensions adjust pension benefits *during* retirement for inflation.
3. State and local government pension plans are excluded from the 1974 law.
4. The lack of "portability" in pensions may result in a reduction in mobility and, for those who move, a reduction in the value of pension rights relative to what the value would be if they did not change jobs (see discussion above).
5. The availability of survivors' benefits remains relatively low, and those benefits paid are often small.
6. Private pension provisions may discourage the hiring of older workers because it typically costs more to provide such workers with a specified pension benefit.

While the drafters of the 1974 private pension legislation admitted in debate that the legislation did not deal with all the problems, they argued that it was a major step forward. And they pointed out that the legislation itself calls for further study of many of the unresolved issues.

What Mix of Public and Private Pensions?

Despite the fact that the first pension plans were established about a century ago, there is still little agreement about the relative virtues of public versus private pensions and what the ideal combination of the two types should be. There is great diversity in the mix of pensions existing in various countries—but there are fewer countries where private programs assume a major role than there are countries that rely primarily on public pensions.

Relatively little has been written that attempts objectively to approach the question of the most desirable pension mix and present data for evaluation purposes. In the United States, the well-known economist Milton Friedman has been a consistent critic of social security and one of the few academics actually to advocate complete abolition of public pensions: "Social Security combines a highly regressive tax with largely indiscriminate benefits and, in overall effect, probably redistributes income from lower to higher income persons. I believe that it serves no essential social function. Existing commitments make it impossible to eliminate it overnight, but it should be unwound and terminated as soon as possible." (Cohen and Friedman, 1972)

There has been very little support for Friedman's rather extreme position. Instead, the more common negative view toward social security has been one that advocates a relatively minor role for it and, consequently, seeks to limit severely any future growth of the program—either by expansion of real benefits or by adding additional functions.

Robert J. Myers, chief actuary for the social security program between 1947 and 1971, labels advocates of a greater role for social security in aged income maintenance as "expansionists" and designates as "moderates" those persons who believe the program should not be expanded. Myers summarizes the moderate viewpoint as one that seeks a governmental program that would provide benefits that would be "sufficient so that, with assests and real estate normally accumulated, the vast majority of beneficiaries will be able to have at least a reasonable subsistence."

Myers (1970) sees social security in the United States at a crossroad:

> It is impossible to predict with any exactitude whether there will be any changes in the relative role of the social security program in our society—and if so, specifically what the changes will be. If the philosophy of moderation largely prevails, the relative role of the social security program will not change significantly. Its provisions will be modified from time to time to keep it up to date and to solve such problems and anomalies as arise, especially those which are not being handled in a reasonably satisfactory manner by the private sector. On the other hand, if the expansionist philosophy prevails, the role of the social security program would be greatly enlarged.*

*See also Myers (1975b).

Over the years concern about an expanded role for social security and rising social security benefits has not been the major issue raised by critics. Rather, most of the concern and criticism has centered on the way benefits have been financed. In Chapter 8, which is devoted exclusively to public and private pension financing, we discuss many of the issues connected with social security financing. In general, the program is criticized because of the heavy tax burden it places on the poor and near-poor and because of the very great differences in contributions paid in versus benefits received among different socioeconomic groups and between the current and future generations.

Criticism of social security, however, has been relatively small in contrast to support voiced for it. On the positive side, three major arguments have been advanced in its favor:

1. That the nonbenefit costs of social insurance are much lower than the costs for *private pension* administration, funds investment, mobility, disclosure to recipients, supervision and regulation, and reinsurance.
2. That it is easier to make social security pensions both inflation proof—adjusting for inflation at and during retirement—and adjustable for economic growth.
3. That it is relatively easy to cover all workers and provide complete portability of credits under social security whereas private pensions present formidable problems in this regard (unless mandated by the government).

Costs   Although social security in the United States is far from being uncomplicated, there are many aspects of its operation that are structured relatively simply. As a consequence, the collection and benefit payout process permits the extensive use of computers. This in turn permits the handling of large numbers of claims in a way that allows significant economies of large-scale operation to be realized. In fiscal year 1974, for example, administrative expenses were only 1.5 percent of OASI payroll contributions.

The issue of comparative costs between social security and private pensions is complicated by the fact that social security financing in the United States is essentially on a pay-as-you-go basis, while private pensions are funded (see Chapter 8). Private pension funding costs generated as a result of financial investment activities carried out on behalf of employers (and, in part, indirectly benefiting the economy) have no analogous counterpart in the United States social security program. Also, another difference between the two types of pensions is the fact that employers and the Internal Revenue Service give lots of "free" administrative services to the social security system.

Insurance companies, unions, corporations, and banks administer private pension plans. Although there has been no study of the comparative costs of private pension plans versus social security, it is hard to imagine that the current conglomeration of thousands of private plans, many covering less than a hundred workers, can have lower administrative costs. A study by Jerry Caswell (1974), for example, of a representative sample of multi-employer plans in the construction industry found that total administrative expenses averaged slightly less than 4 percent of current contributions and that significant economies of scale were associated with larger plans.

Pension Adjustments for Inflation Another important argument made in favor of public pensions is their ability, in contrast to private plans, to deal with the need to respond to inflation and economic growth. The problem of inflation has plagued pension programs since their inception. All countries have had to struggle with this problem, continually adjusting pension programs and benefits to offset increases in price levels. Inflation has varied, for example, from the catastrophic rate in post World War I Germany (which completely wiped out the monetary value of that country's social security reserves and benefits) to the relatively mild price increases averaging less than 2 percent in the United States during the 1958–68 period, to the more than 6 percent per year rate in the United States since 1968.

Gradually most industrialized countries (including the United States in 1972) have introduced some sort of automatic benefit-adjustment mechanisms into the social security program to deal more effectively with the inflation problem. In contrast, private pension plans, with few exceptions, virtually ignore the need for regularized adjustment mechanisms. This results, in large part, because of employers' unwillingness to make financial commitments based on guesses about future price levels and the fear that the cost of these adjustments may be too high.

It is much easier for governments to deal with the inflation problem, given their inherent taxing powers and their ability to minimize the size of the monetary fund necessary to guarantee the financial soundness of the pension program. A pay-as-you-go system, for example, makes it easier to increase revenues to pay for inflation-adjusted wages because the earnings base is also rising with inflation. In contrast, many securities in a reserve fund will not adjust upward in value with the inflation.

The actual history of social security programs in various countries dealing with inflation supports that conclusion; even after runaway inflations, countries have been able to adjust pensions to the new price level. In addition, public pension programs have shown an ability to devise equitable ways of permitting retired persons to share systematically in the real economic growth of the country. Social security programs in some countries—such as Belgium, Canada, Norway, and West Germany—provide for automatic or semiautomatic adjustments in *real* benefit levels. Still others adjust benefits systematically by various ad hoc processes.

Coverage It has proven to be a relatively easy matter in all countries to extend social security coverage to large segments of the labor force. Coverage of agricultural workers and the self-employed has presented problems—especially in developing countries—but, in general, extension of coverage all over the world has been quite comprehensive. In the United States, for example, coverage of the gainfully employed is now very large.

In contrast, extension of private pension coverage presents serious problems. It is especially difficult to extend coverage among small employee groups. Among the factors cited for this difficulty are:

1. The high administrative costs per employee of establishing and maintaining a plan.
2. The lack of pressure from employees or unions.
3. The fact that small business firms are often relatively young and, on average, short-lived.
4. The fact that small employers tend to view pensions as personal costs.
5. The personality of small business owners, who tend to emphasize individual self-reliance in financial matters.

As a result of these and other factors, a sizable proportion of the work force in countries with private pensions may not be covered by such pensions.

In fact, this is the actual case in the United States. Estimates of private pension coverage are subject to a wide margin of error. Recent estimates of the proportion of workers covered have varied from 35 to 50 percent. The best study thus far available is for "full-time employees" only (in 1972) and reports 47 percent coverage—with coverage for men being 52 percent and coverage for women being much lower at 36 percent. Based on this study and other information, the Social Security Administration estimates that 44 percent of private wage and salary workers were covered by private pension plans in 1973.

One possible solution to the coverage problem is for the government to require that all employers provide private pension benefits.

Some countries have done this. Great Britain, for example, is in the process of implementing such a requirement to provide pensions as supplements to social security. British employers must privately provide pension protection equal to government minimums or contribute to a quasi-public funded pension scheme.

Arguments in Support of Private Pensions

Given the arguments advanced in favor of social security pensions, what arguments are made to support the existence and expansion of private pensions? There are two major ones:

1. That social security—because of its broad coverage—must remain very uniform in its benefit provisions, while private pensions are flexible and can be tailored to meet differing situations and conditions (e.g., hazardous conditions) of various industries, particular firms, or different occupational groups.
2. That private pensions are vital to assure the saving necessary to provide sufficient investment in a growing economy.

Flexibility   On the one hand, a private pension can be a flexible management tool. As Charles A. Siegfried (1970) of the Metropolitan Life Insurance Company has observed, "a pension plan can be devised to attract and hold employees or it can be devised to facilitate the separation of employees from employment." On the other hand, pension objectives may vary to accommodate different employee wishes and aspirations, these being determined by decisions of the employers (unilaterally or in consultation with workers) or by collective bargaining.

The late Edwin S. Hewitt, a well-known pension consultant, arguing the case for private pensions before the U.S. Senate Special Committee on Aging, emphasized the flexibility factor:

It is extraordinary how flexible an instrument for providing adequate security the private plan has proved to be. There are two kinds of flexibility and perhaps this fact is underrated when we oppose what private plans are doing.

First, is their flexibility in terms of adapting to different needs. Very real differences in security problems exist among different companies, different industries, different age groups...

The second dimension is the flexibility between periods of time. Private plans have exhibited amazing flexibility to make their provisions meet the different needs that a group may have at different times.

The initial job of most pension plans when first established is to concentrate on retirement income for the older worker, hence the importance of past service benefits.* As plans become better funded, they tend to branch into other areas. Variety increases as plans are able to spend more money and give attention to tailormade benefits to meet specific needs. (Hewitt, 1970)

Pension Saving and Capital Formation   A much more controversial argument made in favor of private pensions is their role in the mobilization of national saving for economic investment. Charles Moeller, an economist for the Metropolitan Life Insurance Company, has argued the positive aspects this way:

> The key to any nation's economic growth is its ability to direct substantial portions of its output into real investment, i.e., to defer current consumption of output through saving and to permit investment in *productive* facilities for use in future production processes.... In effect, what pension funding operations and other forms of contractual saving do is to improve the efficiency and stability of the capital markets....
> The importance of the saving function for private pension plans cannot be too strongly emphasized. The need for encouraging the accumulation of individual saving flows and of recirculating these funds back into the economy through the investment process has been spotlighted by the dramatic events of recent years including the "crunch" of 1966 and the "liquidity crisis" of 1970. (Moeller, 1972)

While there is wide agreement that there is a need for saving in an economy, there are a variety of ways such saving can be accumulated and, hence, no agreement on the need or importance of any one accumulation process—such as through private pensions. In the key growth sector of *corporate* production, the overwhelming majority of funds needed to finance new investment comes from the *internal* funds saved by the corporations themselves. As John Kenneth Galbraith has observed, "The decisions on what will be saved are made in the main by a few hundred large corporations." Other possible sources of saving are unincorporated business, individuals, and government budget surpluses.

Moreover, there is disagreement over the extent to which there is any insufficiency of saving in the United States relative to investment opportunities and the willingness of business to undertake investment. Bosworth, Duesenberry and Carron (1975), for example, predict no short run shortages in their study *Capital Needs in the Seventies.*

---

*Past service benefits are credits for years of work in the firm prior to the establishment of the pension plan. Most benefit formulas pay benefits that rise with years of service with the company.

Economists Martin Feldstein (1975) and Alicia Munnell (1974) have recently presented evidence that indicates growing social security benefits are reducing total personal savings. On the other hand, economist Arthur Okun (1975) has recently observed that "the specter of depressed saving is not only empirically implausible but logically fake.... The nation can have the level of saving and investment it wants with more or less [income] redistribution, so long as it is willing to twist some other dials."

Finally, it should be noted that the generation of savings through pensions is not limited to private pensions. Public social security reserve funds can also be generated. For example, the financing rates for the social security program in Sweden have been deliberately set high enough to help the chronic shortage of savings in the Swedish economy. In fact, public pension reserves may be a particularly attractive means of mobilizing saving in developing countries where private pensions are virtually nonexistent.

The Pension Mix in Various Countries

If we look at the pension programs currently existing in various industrialized countries, we find that there is a tendency to rely heavily either on public pensions or on some sort of private/public combination *with extensive regulation of the private sector*. In countries that rely heavily on private pensions, the tendency is for the private and public pension programs to be closely coordinated by a large number of complex legislative and administrative mechanisms and regulations. In France, for example, it is difficult to make a distinction between social security and the widespread private pension programs—given the elaborate coordinating mechanisms that have been established.

In the United States, both public and private pension plans have assumed a growing share of responsibility for providing retirement income needs. The indications are that this collective share will continue to grow. But it is not yet clear how that responsibility will be ultimately divided.

Government Employee Pension Plans

Our discussion of pension plans would not be complete without mentioning one other category. In addition to social security and private pensions there are federal, state, and local plans for government employees. These plans have many characteristics similar to the public and private plans discussed above but are unique in some respects.

Most civilians working for the federal government are covered by the civil service retirement pension program. In 1973 there were 3.7 million beneficiaries receiving about $15 billion in pension, survivor, and disability benefits under this program. (Dales, 1975) Benefits are computed on the basis of length of service and the average of the highest three consecutive years of earnings. An automatic cost-of-living adjustment is made to this benefit.

While federal civilian employees are not covered by social security, the relatively low number of quarters needed to qualify for social security in the past has encouraged them to seek dual coverage. Many federal employees work part-time while employed by the government and/or retire (perhaps early) from government employment, take a new job to obtain social security eligibility, and eventually obtain a minimum (or better) social security benefit. In fact, the U.S. Joint Economic Committee estimated in 1973 that 40 percent of all civil service pensioners also received social security pensions. (Storey, 1973)

The cost and inequity of providing social security benefits to federal pensioners has been condemned by many, and the most recent Social Security Advisory Council recommended mandatory social security coverage for all government employees.

State and local pension plans are similar in many ways to private employer plans. James A. Maxwell (1975) has summarized some of the differences:

> Overall, the state and local government pension systems provide more generous benefits than do private systems. The normal retirement age and service requirements are more generous.... And they are more likely to have generous disability and survivor coverage. Most state and local government pensions are based on final average pay... [Most] require employee contributions, whereas most private plans do not.

Tilove's recent study (1976) of state and local plans finds two other important differences between private and public employee plans. In a sharp reversal from previous studies, Tilove finds that vesting provisions are now somewhat more prevalent in public than in private plans. And, while automatic post-retirement benefit adjustments are almost nonexistent in private plans, they "are the most recent and most rapidly expanding changes among public systems." Currently a little over half of all state and local employees are covered by some sort of automatic adjustment mechanism when they retire.

Various amendments to the Social Security Act have permitted state and local governments to cover their employees by social security. Close to two-thirds of state and local employees, consequently, are concurrently covered by both social security and a state or local pension plan. Again, for workers not covered by social security, dual coverage is often achieved by early retirement from state or local service followed by work for a nongovernment employer.

Benefits are typically very good under state and local plans; Tilove (1976) reports that in the future "many public employees will be retiring with more net income than while they were working." These high benefits have resulted in considerable concern about the rising costs of these benefits and the way state and local governments are planning (or, some would say, not planning) to finance them. It is to this question of pension financing that we now turn.

Suggested Readings

Ball, Robert M. "Social Security and Private Pension Plans." *National Tax Journal* (September 1974): 467–471.
>A former commissioner of Social Security argues that the role of social security should be increased but explains why he also feels that the role of private pensions will not diminish significantly in the near future.
Bernstein, Merton. *The Future of Private Pensions.* New York: Free Press, 1964.
>Despite its date, this book is a useful introduction to the various aspects of private pensions. Bernstein emphasizes the lack of portability and the inflation problems associated with private pensions and argues for the development of a workable portability mechanism.
Bleakney, Thomas P. *Retirement Systems for Public Employees.* Homewood, Ill.: Irwin, 1972.
>Written by a consulting actuary, this book focuses on the design and administration of public retirement systems. The author discusses alternative financing procedures and stresses the importance of identifying the real costs over the long run of retirement provisions when first enacted.
Lesnoy, Selig D., and John C. Hambor. "Social Security, Saving, and Capital Formation." *Social Security Bulletin* 38 (July 1975): 3–15.
>An explanation for noneconomists of the relationship of social security to saving and capital formation. A variety of relevant data and recent research findings are summarized.
McGill, Dan M. *Fundamentals of Private Pensions*, 3rd ed. Homewood, Ill.: Irwin, 1975.
>A comprehensive and authoritative book that traces the historical development and regulation of private pensions, explains plan design, reviews funding procedures, and discusses actuarial practices.

Paul, Robert D. "Can Private Pension Plans Deliver?" *Harvard Business Review* (September–October 1974):22 ff.
A pension consultant's view of the history of pension plans and the future pressures and problems that require the development of new types of plans. Inflation considerations and unisex plans receive special attention.

Schulz, James H. *Pension Aspects of the Economics of Aging: Present and Future Roles of Private Pensions.* U.S. Senate Special Committee on Aging Committee Print. 91st Congress, 2nd session. Washington, D.C.: U.S. Government Printing Office, 1970.
A review of pension developments up to 1970 and a discussion of various key issues. The study includes a discussion of conflicts in plan purposes and seeks to explain some myths associated with private pensions.

Taggart, Robert. *The Labor Market Impacts of the Private Retirement System.* In Subcommittee on Fiscal Policy, U.S. Joint Economic Committee. *Studies in Public Welfare.* Paper No. 11. Washington, D.C.: U.S. Government Printing Office, 1973.
An analytical review of research investigating the impact of private pensions on labor mobility and employment.

Tilove, Robert. *Public Employee Pension Funds.* © Twentieth Century Fund. New York: Columbia University Press, 1976.
A study of 129 of the largest state and local retirement systems, covering (in 1972) about 70 percent of all employees in such plans. In addition to simply surveying plan characteristics, Tilove presents a comprehensive and careful analysis of many important pension issues, including the relationship between social security and public employee plans.

Chapter Eight

Pension Financing:
Who Pays?
Who Should Pay?

In an article entitled "The Young Pay for the Old," journalist Edwin L. Dale, Jr. (1973), wrote:

> A funny thing happened to your taxes on the way to 1973. Congress passed the biggest federal increase since the Korean war (and that one was temporary), and hardly anybody peeped except a few intellectuals. This was happening at the time of the "taxpayers' revolt" at federal, state, and local levels. It was at the time when even George Wallace was appealing to a sense of frustration in the middle and lower middle classes, telling them the tax system was unfair. It was an election year....
>
> Before anyone wonders whether he missed some important news development, or has been somehow bamboozled, it is best to explain the mystery. The paradox is resolved in two words: social security...a $7-billion tax increase enacted in 1972 with scarcely a voice of protest.*

One of the most important, but until recently one of the least controversial, aspects of pension policy among the public has been the way these programs were financed. Few people realize the magnitude of the expenditures involved in pension programs and hence the tremendously large amount of funds that must be raised through taxes, worker "contributions," and employer allocations for pension purposes. In 1973, $79 billion in pension benefits were paid to Americans (see Table 18). This amount, by way of comparison, was $5 billion *more* than national defense expenditures in the same year; about $13 billion less than total business investment; and almost equal to the entire consumer population's expenditures that year on automobiles, gasoline, and oil.

* © 1973 by The New York Times Company. Reprinted by permission.

Table 18   Pension Expenditures, 1973

	Billions
OASI Benefits	$ 43.7
Private Pension and Deferred Profit-Sharing Plan Benefits .	$ 11.2
Contributions Paid into Pension Reserves . . . . $ 21.1	
Pension Reserves, Book Value. $180.2	
Federal Employee Pension Benefits.	$ 9.7
Veterans' Pensions and Compenstaion	$ 6.4
State and Local Government Pension Plan Benefits	$ 5.5
Railroad Retirement Benefits	$ 2.6
Benefit Total	$ 79.1

Sources: "Current Operating Statistics," in *Social Security Bulletin* (July 1975); W.W. Koldrubetz, "Employee-Benefit Plans, 1973," *Social Security Bulletin* (May 1975): 26; Sophie R. Dales, "Benefits and Beneficiaries Under Public Employee Retirement Systems, Calendar Year 1973," Research and Statistics Note No. 21-1974 (Washington, D.C.: Social Security Administration, 1974).

And, in order to meet *future* expenditure obligations, private pension funds currently have amassed over $200 billion in financial assets.

In recent years, there has been a sharp increase in criticisms of pension financing techniques—especially those used for social security. Pension financing involves many complex issues and, no doubt, part of the recent controversy engendered by the topic arises because of the confusion and misunderstanding that generally prevail. Is the social security system bankrupt, as is frequently charged? Will younger workers get back less than they contribute to social security? Who pays for private pensions—the employer by tax-subsidized expense write-offs or the worker as a result of reduced take-home pay? Do public and private pension financing burdens fall disproportionately on the poor and treat racial minorities and women unfairly?

We will divide the discussion of pension financing into four broad aspects: (a) current social security financing practices and the role of pension plan reserves, (b) the equity of present practices, (c) a review of various proposed changes in how social security financing should be carried out, and (d) the financing of private and state/local government pensions.

Financing Social Security

The OASDHI program is financed by a payroll tax that requires that workers in covered employment (regardless of age) pay a percent of their earnings into the program and that employers pay an equivalent percentage based on their employees' earnings.* In both cases the percentage paid is limited to the earnings of each employee up to a specified maximum. In the original legislation (and up to 1949) this maximum, called the *earnings base*, was $3000. Between 1950 and 1972 the earnings base was increased periodically on an ad hoc basis. Then in 1972, legislation was passed that set the earnings base at $12,000 in 1974 and specified that the base was henceforth to rise *automatically* as average earnings rose. By 1976 the earnings base had reached $15,300, resulting in an $895 payment by workers at or over the base.

J. Douglas Brown (1972) writes that "as originally enacted, the old age insurance system would have accumulated in time a reserve of $47 billion, more than the outstanding debt of the government in 1935." But before any benefits were actually paid by the new pension program, Congress quickly revised the contribution rates, postponing scheduled increases in the payroll tax. This action set the pattern for future financing action, with tax rates being set below the rates that would be appropriate for a private pension or insurance plan.

Over the years there has been considerable controversy over whether "adequate" financing of social insurance programs requires the accumulation of large financial reserves. A major part of the discussion has centered on the extent to which public insurance programs require financing practices conforming to the traditional tenets of actuarial soundness associated with private insurance.

The term "actuarial soundness" refers to the ability of insurance programs to provide sufficient (i.e., legally obligated) payments to eligible recipients at the time they come due. A private insurance company, for example, must necessarily operate on the basis that it will not sell any new policies in the future. Therefore, it should always have sufficient funds on hand to meet its obligations for existing policyholders, even if they all surrender their policies at once. Similarly, private pension plans generally try to maintain reserve funds sufficient to meet current contracted obligations but, at the same time, often amortize (i.e., pay over a period of years, usually 10 or more) the cost of benefits provided for employee services rendered *before the pension plan began operation*.

There is now widely accepted agreement among pension specialists that social security programs do *not* require the accumulation of large amounts of reserves to be actuarially sound. (*See*, for example, Myers (1975a), Chapter 4) It is recognized that the taxing power of the government helps to guarantee the long-run financial integrity of such programs and that, unlike private insurance, it is appropriate to assume

*The social security payroll tax rates at the time of writing (1976) were 5.85 percent each for employer and employee and 7.9 percent for the self-employed.

that the programs will operate indefinitely—with a consequent continuous flow of revenue. And perhaps more fundamentally, the fact that public insurance is usually compulsory and covers most of the population avoids the financing problems arising from a fluctuating number of participants.

Financing social security this way is commonly referred to as the pay-as-you-go method. Benefits are paid to the current aged out of the payroll tax contributions of the current working population. In return, members of the working population know that they are promised benefits when they become eligible, financed out of the taxes of the future working population.

Thus, while social security reserves have increased in 30 out of 37 years (1937–1974), total reserves in 1974 were equal to less than one year's disbursement (76 percent of 1974 benefits). Given this small reserve, some people have argued erroneously that social security is a bankrupt program that does not have the money to pay its obligations. Without necessarily characterizing the situation as bankruptcy, others have seriously questioned the financial soundness of the program. For example, an August 23, 1974, editorial in the *Wall Street Journal* argued in part:

> And unless we are mistaken, the system is not financially sound in its present form.
> The one number that jars us, more than any other, is that as of June 30, 1973, the net unfunded liability of the system was $2.1 trillion. What this means is that current members of the system, working and retired, have been promised $2.1 trillion more—in constant dollars—than they will henceforth pay into the system.

As we indicated above, the unfunded liability results in part from a decision by Congress not to operate a funded system. Part of the unfunded liability arises, however, from a related decision to grant significant pension benefits to persons reaching retirement age during the initial years of the program ("blanketing in"). To become eligible for social security benefits an individual must work a certain number of calendar quarters. With regard to this older worker group, the Congress set the required quarters very low, which resulted in their receiving benefits that far exceeded their few years of contributions.

Thus, ever since the social security system began, most retirees have received more benefits than they have paid in. New groups that become covered in the fifties and sixties also were granted these "windfall gains." And with liberalizations in the benefit structure, without commensurate increases in taxes, most retirees still, and for many years to come, will also experience these gains.

This policy—*not* to exclude persons with relatively few years of participation in the program and *not* to make them "pay their way"—has been financed on a pay-as-you-go basis out of the rising earnings of the working population with only modest increases in taxes. But it has also added to the "unfunded" liabilities of the social security program.

In answer to critics of these nonfunding practices, five former secretaries of the Department of Health, Education, and Welfare and three former Social Security commissioners issued on February 10, 1975, a statement emphasizing why the government need not amass vast reserves to keep social security financially sound. In part, they argued:

> By earmarking the proceeds of social security taxes for the payment of benefits and depositing them in a trust fund for this purpose, by entitling the system insurance, by continuing actions to assure its financial soundness, and by innumerable pronouncements of congressional committees and individual spokesmen, Congress has made clear beyond question its pledge to the American people that the social security commitment will be honored.

Thus, we see that the main argument for nonfunding rests on the quality of the promise made by the government. To fulfill this promise requires that social security planning insure that over the long run the flow of funds remains in a "satisfactory actuarial status."

But what constitutes satisfactory actuarial status? A recent Panel on Social Security Financing—composed of economists and actuaries—argued that this means being able to predict with reasonable confidence (a) that future scheduled income and future scheduled outgo will be in harmony, and (b) that future scheduled taxes required to support the program be within the limits of practical acceptability to the social security tax-paying population. (U.S. Senate Finance Committee, 1975)

Actuarial projections of future benefits and taxes are made annually by the Social Security Administration's Office of the Actuary. The projections and a general assessment of financial status are submitted in a report by the Social Security Board of Trustees to Congress each year. Up until recently there had been little concern expressed in these reports about any long-term financing problem. In the 1974 report, however, the actuarial projection forecast a significant actuarial deficit over the 75-year period 1974–2048. This projected deficit, higher than any previously forecasted, *was almost doubled one year later* when the trustees issued their 1975 report!

This long-term financing problem is caused by three major factors: (a) the post–World War II "baby boom," (b) the dramatic decline in recent years of the birthrate and (c) expanding pension expenditures arising from the automatic cost-of-living adjustment mechanism legislated in 1972.

Figure 10 shows the birthrate in the United States over the 1935–1973 period. The steady rise in births after World War II (reaching a peak in 1957) results in a rising ratio of the retirement-age population to the working-age population beginning about the year 2010, when the "baby-boom" population reaches old age. The drop in the birthrate in recent years causes the rise in the ratio to be even sharper, since the falling number of births reduces the number of persons who will be in the future working population.

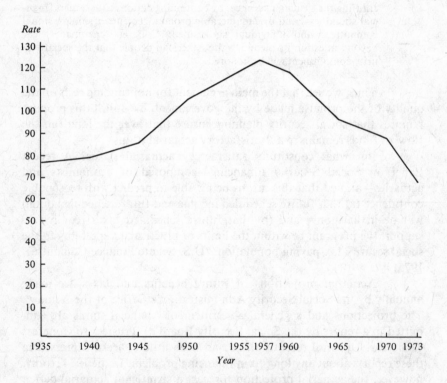

Figure 10.   General Birthrate in the United States, 1935–1973

Source: U.S. Bureau of the Census, *Current Population Reports,* Series P-25, No. 521, "Estimates of the Population of the United States and Components of Change, 1973, with Annual Data from 1930" (Washington, D.C.: U.S. Government Printing Office, 1974).

The third reason why actuarial deficits were projected to increase relates to *the particular way* the 1972 legislation specified that pension benefits were to be automatically adjusted for inflation. Soon after this change, various pension analysts demonstrated that the particular inflation adjustment mechanism legislated had the unintended effect of increasing the *real* value of benefits for workers retiring in future years. The greater the rate of inflation, the greater the increase in real benefits, and hence the greater the future financial burden on social security.*

When the 1972 legislation was passed, much lower inflation rates were anticipated than characterized subsequent years, and it is clear that Congress did not fully understand the extreme sensitivity of the mechanism they adopted to general economic conditions. By the time the Advisory Council on Social Security met in 1974, this adjustment problem was recognized, and it became the central issue to which the council gave its attention. The council recommended that the adjustment mechanism be changed so that automatic increases in real benefit levels would not occur and showed that much lower social security costs would occur in the future if such a change were made.

It is likely that the automatic adjustment mechanism will be changed. If it is, however, it will not completely solve the long-term social security cost problems. The two demographic factors will remain.

Thus, there is no doubt that the costs of social security will continue to rise over time and that the government is faced with the problem of finding the best means of raising the additional funds. Of course, an alternative way of dealing with the problem would be to reduce benefit levels and/or to raise the eligibility age for beginning to receive benefits.†￼ It is not very likely that future advisory groups will propose a general reduction in social security benefits, but the 1974 Advisory Council on Social Security did recommend that future consideration be given to increasing the social security eligibility age.

Neither of these two alternatives appears likely—not only because of past promises made and the political and moral issues they raise, but also because of the general low level of current benefits; for large numbers of older persons benefit levels fail to meet rising expectations with regard to what is considered "adequate" income in retirement.

---

*We do not present the relatively technical explanation for this result. Interested readers should see the monograph by Lawrence Thompson listed in the Suggested Readings at the end of this chapter.

†It is also technically possible to *raise* (rather than *reduce*) benefit levels but at a rate that would result in a decline in the pension/earnings ratio (i.e., the replacement rate).

However, there is a related change that *is* likely to take place. The current discrimination against older workers and the various encouragements for their early retirement will probably moderate. This change in manpower attitudes has already occurred in Europe. Many European countries have experienced a "demographic bulge" problem similar to the one facing the United States. Their bulge is primarily a result of the high loss of young males during World War II. As a consequence, *these countries have had to impose much higher tax rates but also have had generally more liberal policies to encourage workers to remain in the labor force.* The United States is likely eventually to develop similar policies.

Financing Equity

Rising costs of social security now and in the future increase the importance of developing financing methods considered fair by the population. A good question to begin with in assessing the equity of social security is "who pays?" In the United States, the size of the payroll tax exceeds all other federal, state, and local types of taxes except the federal income tax. Thus, it is important to look at who pays the tax and the relationship between those taxes paid and the benefits ultimately received.

Who Pays? Determining "tax incidence" or who ultimately bears the burden of any tax is one of the most complex issues in economics. While the general population thinks it knows who "pays" taxes, economists disagree—especially about who actually bears the corporate income tax, sales taxes, and the property tax. Until recently, the payroll tax had received little attention from economists. While most people have assumed the worker bears the burden of *his* payroll contribution, there has been great disagreement over the employer payments. A variety of recent economic studies indicate that most of the employer tax is ultimately paid by the worker in the form of wages that are lower than what they otherwise would have been (or, to a smaller extent, by consumers in the form of higher prices). In the most thorough study of the question to date, economist John A. Brittain's findings indicate that the worker generally bears all the tax. He found that given the level of productivity, the higher the employer payroll tax rate the lower the basic real wage—the wage rate being lower by the same amount as the payroll tax increase. (Brittain, 1972)

The payroll tax has been criticized as unfair by numerous people. There have been three major criticisms: (a) that the tax is regressive and a heavy burden on the poor, (b) that the tax is unfair to certain groups of beneficiaries, given the benefits they are likely to receive, and (c) that younger workers who are now paying taxes (and those in the future) are likely to get an "unfair deal." We will examine each of these criticisms in turn.

First, the issue of a regressive tax structure and its impact on the poor: In general a regressive tax is one where the amount of tax paid is a *declining* proportion of income as incomes *increase*. Since the payroll tax is levied only on the "earnings base" and not on earnings above the maximum earnings ceiling, the tax is partly regressive. The proportion that contributions represent of total earnings falls *for earnings levels above the ceiling*.

During the fifties and sixties the maximum ceiling was low relative to average earnings. The proportion of total earnings in covered employment subject to the payroll tax fell from more than 90 percent during the early years of the program to a low of 71 percent in 1965. Thus, for example, in 1972, when the earnings base was $9000, about one-quarter of the workers paying social security taxes had earnings that exceeded the maximum. With the significant increase and indexing of the earnings ceiling that began in 1973, the proportion of total earnings in covered employment has risen to 82 percent in 1973.

What concerns many critics, however, is not the burden on workers with earnings near or above the maximum. They are concerned more about the taxes paid by low wage earners. For example, on October 4, 1972, a group of economists at the prestigious Brookings Institution wrote to the *Washington Post* to protest the payroll tax:

> The rise of the payroll tax has been a quiet drain on low- and middle-income Americans. For the middle-income workers, payroll tax increases have more than offset the much vaunted reductions of personal income taxes of 1964, 1969, and 1971. . . .
>
> For low-income workers earning $3000, payroll tax increases have exceeded personal tax cuts. A worker with two or more dependents who is employed year round at the minimum wage is spared personal income tax because of his poverty, but he will pay $176 in payroll taxes himself in 1973 under present law; his employer also pays $176 . . .

Why should people with poverty-level incomes have to pay any taxes—including social security?

The principal answer given by supporters of the current payroll tax is that the benefit structure of the program is heavily weighted in favor of low earners and that tampering with the tax structure threatens to turn the program into a welfare program—thereby undermining its general political acceptability. J. Douglas Brown in a memorandum sent to the U.S. Senate Special Committee on Aging (1973) gives some additional arguments:

> Overall, the advantages of uniform proportionate contributions toward one's social insurance protection are of great psychological, social and political importance. They clearly differentiate benefits as a matter of right from those available only on individual proof of need. They reflect a natural desire for self-reliance. They refute a criticism of dependency. They also are a factor in avoiding a class-conscious society in which some classes give and some classes get. Proportionate contributions are a force for political restraint in the evolution of a total system, both in respect to excessive demands for liberality in the benefit structure and the condoning of abuses in unwarranted payments.

As the costs of social security rise and the burdens on low earners also rise, however, the pressures for reform will no doubt increase, despite the strong historical resistance to changing the taxing structure. We will discuss a number of reform proposals in a section to follow, but first let us examine the other two major equity issues raised at the beginning of this section.

Intergenerational Equity   From time to time people argue, and sometimes present calculations to show, that payments to social security by new entrants into the labor force will be much greater than the retirement benefits they can expect to receive subsequently. *Such calculations almost always assume that currently legislated contribution rates and benefit levels will remain unchanged in the future*, which is an unrealistic assumption.

A better way to investigate this question is to calculate "lifetime rates of return." This method mathematically determines the rate of interest or rate of return implicity earned on payroll tax contributions paid over a worker's lifetime. It is done by comparing the taxes paid (plus an imputed interest rate on them) to the benefits received during the entire retirement period. John Brittain, using 1966 tax and benefit levels, estimated projected yields for *average* earners that ranged from about 3 to 6 percent, depending on assumptions with regard to economic growth, birth/mortality rates, the interest rate, and the age when entering the work force. Brittain (1972) concluded that "if the model and the official demographic projections are fairly realistic, new contributors will in the aggregate get neither a very good 'buy' nor a very bad one, but they will fare moderately well." A more recent study by Chen and Chu of 1974 retirees and entrants calculates similar lifetime rates of return. The rates for 1974 *retirees* range from 6 to almost 17 percent. Entrants into the labor force in 1974 are estimated to have much lower rates of return, between 1 and 8 percent. (Chen and Chu, 1974)

The wide range of rates of return estimated by Brittain and more recently by Chen and Chu demonstrates the difficulty of giving an unequivocal answer to the question of whether social security is a "good buy"; results are highly sensitive to the assumptions made in the analysis. Also, both studies fail to include in the analysis federal and state income tax treatments of contributions and benefits. And as Brittain (1972) has argued, "Why should one ask whether a person ultimately recoups in benefits the equivalent of his taxes when the same question is rarely asked about other taxes?...Since the taxes and later benefits assigned to a person are not at all closely related, as they are under private insurance, a strong case can be made for completely separate analysis and evaluation of the tax and benefit structures on their own merits."

Examination of the findings from the Brittain and Chen/Chu studies does effectively spotlight possible differences between various population groups. Brittain, for example, notes that the wide spread in the rates of return indicates substantial income redistribution among categories of participants. For example, the college graduate who starts work at 22 fares much better than the high school graduate who starts work at 18 if both earn the same average earnings over their respective work lives. Their social security benefits will be very similar, but the college graduate, entering the work force later, will pay less total payroll taxes over his career.

Women and Social Security Financing   Certain specific groups have been singled out for special attention by some critics of social security. The treatment of women has recently come under careful scrutiny.* In the financing area the most controversial issue has been the differential treatment of working and nonworking women. Currently, a spouse is entitled to a benefit equal to 50 percent of the working partner's pension—regardless of whether or not they themselves participate in the social security program. A spouse who works, however, may become eligible for a regular benefit on the basis of that work. The law stipulates that such a person can get only one benefit—50 percent of their spouse's pension or their own pension, whichever is larger.

*See, for example, the report of the Task Force on Women and Social Security listed in the Suggested Readings at the end of this chapter.

The issue that arises from this treatment of working spouses is whether it is fair for the family where both work to pay more social security taxes than a family with only one wage earner. A two-worker family will pay combined social security taxes that are greater than a one-worker family with the same earnings, but in relation to the benefits of the single-worker family, the two-worker family:

1. May receive the *same* retirement benefits, if the spouse doesn't work a sufficient number of quarters to achieve eligibility.
2. May receive *more* retirement benefits, if the spouse achieves eligibility and has earnings that result in entitlement to a benefit greater than 50 percent of the spouse's benefit.
3. May receive *fewer* retirement benefits, because of anomalies in the benefit structure that, for example, in 1975 resulted in benefits of $457 per month if each spouse had average annual earnings of $4000 but $474.50 if one worker had average annual earnings of $8000 and a spouse receiving a spouse benefit.*

While a working woman may receive little or no more retirement benefits than a nonworking spouse, she does receive certain protection under social security not available to a nonworking wife:

1. Disability protection.
2. Benefits payable at or after age 62, even if her husband continues to work.
3. Monthly benefits to her children if she becomes disabled or dies.

The economic role of women has been shifting over time. (See Kahne, 1975) As a result, a number of social security reform bills have been introduced in Congress over the years to deal, for example, with the working woman issue. Thus far, however, no serious consideration has been given to legislation on this matter. This issue and other matters, such as whether to have social security benefits for housewives, are likely to be hotly debated in the years to come. As Rita Campbell argued in a dissenting opinion when the Advisory Council on Social Security (1975) recommended no major action in this area:

It is my belief that because of the continuing trends in the increasing labor force participation rate of women, the declining labor force participation rate of men, the increase in divorce and decrease in marriages, and the decline in the birth rate, it is advisable to begin now to restructure the social security system to adapt to these socioeconomic changes rather than wait for dissatisfaction with the system to so increase as to force hurried changes which may be undesirable.

*The example is cited by Rita R. Campbell in Advisory Council on Social Security (1975).

Differential Life Expectancies

Another issue that has been raised in relation to women and also by various ethnic minority groups is the extent to which differences in average life expectancy should be taken into account. Women, *on average*, tend to live longer than men; nonwhites, *on average*, have shorter life expectancies than whites. For benefit purposes, social security policy has largely ignored these or any other differences in life expectancies. Some private pensions, however, *have* paid differential pension benefits based on sex, causing certain women's organizations to challenge in the courts such differentials in benefits.

In contrast, some nonwhites argue that they *should* receive preferential social security benefits because of adverse life expectancy rates. For example, the 1971 White House Conference on Aging "special concerns session" on aged blacks recommended: "The minimum age-eligibility requirement for primary beneficiaries of Old Age, Survivors, Disability, and Health Insurance (OASDHI under social security) should be reduced by 8 years for black males so as to erase existing racial inequities."

The average life expectancy *at birth* is different for whites versus nonwhites, in large part because of higher infant mortality rates for nonwhites. However, differences in life expectancies at other ages are not nearly as great (See the tables in the appendix to Chapter 2). At age 65, for example, there are almost no differences.

Ubadigbo Okonkwo has recently investigated "Intragenerational Equity Under Social Security" for subgroups of the United States population differentiated by race, marital status, education, and region of residence. Calculating "internal rates of return" by race, Okonwo finds that returns are higher for all groups of nonwhite workers except nonwhite couples with 16 or more years of schooling. The highly favorable mortality experience of white female college graduates results in a more favorable internal rate of return for these couples.

Okonkwo (1975) concludes:

> In general, the progressivity of the social security benefit structure tended to redistribute lifetime earnings in favor of subgroups with low earnings, exemplified by nonwhites and workers with relatively few years of schooling. However, this redistributive effect was weakened, but not reversed, by the relatively smaller probabilities of survival experienced by these subgroups. . . .

Viscusi and Zeckhauser (1976) in their book *Welfare of the Elderly* argue against public pension differentials based on life expectancy. They cite the widespread resentment that would probably be generated by an explicit set of different eligibility criteria or benefit levels. And they point out the administrative and practical difficulties in taking account of all differentials—smokers versus nonsmokers, drivers of safer cars, persons in occupations or industries with environmental settings that may affect health. Finally, they argue that these differentials are not as important as equalizing benefits per unit of need. "Once we accept the notion that the principal focus of Social Security should be on equalizing income for the periods one is alive, the need to adjust for differing lengths of lifetimes is not only unnecessary, but is is also detrimental to this more fundamental objective."

Reform Proposals

Numerous proposals for changing the financing of social security have been put forth. This section will look at only three approaches: (a) the Buchanan proposal to change radically social security, (b) general revenue financing, and (c) changing the payroll tax structure.

The Buchanan Proposal Economists James Buchanan and Colin Campbell have written about the inequities they see arising from the social security system. They proposed in an article published in the *Wall Street Journal* that a new system of financing be devised that would, in effect, finance the "windfall gains benefits" of current and future social security recipients out of general revenue.* Once this is done, they recommend that the payroll tax be set at a rate that would make it certain (actuarially) that the amount persons paid in to the program would equal, on average, the amount that is paid out to them.

In a later article Buchanan amplified the original proposal, calling for a radical change in the social security structure. According to him, the purpose of the proposed new program is "to embody the advantages of an intergenerational tax transfer program while at the same time incorporating most of the desirable features of a genuine insurance program." (Buchanan, 1968)

Buchanan's statement refers to the advantages of an intergenerational tax transfer program. As originally described by economist Paul Samuelson (1958), there can be a "subsidy" in public social security programs that moves from one generation to the next as a result of population growth and economic growth in the economy. Buchanan seeks to

---

*We discuss in a later section of this chapter the matter of windfall gains and the issue of general revenue financing.

establish a social security program that would embody that subsidy advantage but, at the same time, be more consistent with private insurance principles in terms of a *guaranteed* pension payoff based upon law.

Buchanan proposes that the present payroll tax be repealed. In its place, individuals would be required to purchase "social insurance bonds." The pension benefits being paid out at any particular time would be financed from revenues (purchases) of bonds sold during the same period.

Thus, when someone bought a bond for retirement, the money that the individual pays out would be immediately transferred to people who were currently retired. This would be similar to the current practice of taking social security contributions and immediately paying them out to current social security pension recipients. If these bond revenues were insufficient to meet current benefit obligations, Buchanan proposes that general revenue financing be used to pay for the balance of benefits due. In this way, he argues, current bond purchasers would not be paying for the results of blanketing in certain groups (see p. 136) or for higher individual benefits that are not based upon prior contributions.

If they wanted to, individuals would be allowed (under Buchanan's plan) to buy more bonds than the compulsory amount. *In either case, however, individuals would be able to buy bonds from either private companies or government.* When the individual turns 65, the bonds mature, and he can then convert them into an annuity.

As far as the government bonds are concerned, Buchanan proposes that the return on them be the higher of the following: either the interest rate on long-term U.S. Treasury bonds or the rate of growth of the nation's total economic output (gross national product). As a result, the private bonds—in order to compete—would have to promise (with a fair degree of certainty) a rate of return either better than the interest rate on long-term government bonds (if one didn't expect any growth in the economy) or equal to the rate of general growth in the economy.

Thus, we see that Buchanan accepts the need for compulsory pension programs. And he also agrees that there need not be reserve funding—accepting the validity of a nonfunded, pay-as-you-go government program. But he seeks by his proposal to prevent inequities that occur as a result of combining liabilities resulting from newly covered beneficiaries or "new" benefits to old beneficiaries (retroactive benefits) with liabilities based upon payments made by individuals over their lifetimes.

Buchanan tries to incorporate into the system an adjustment procedure that guarantees that the individual in the social security system will benefit from the general growth of the economy. Adjusting the bonds at the same rate as the changing gross national product also takes care of the problem of inflation. If one adjusts the bond rate to the rate of growth of money gross national product, this will automatically adjust for general price increases in the economy. Thus, one would have both a price-adjustment and a real-growth-adjustment factor built into the social security system.

Buchanan argues that such a program would have much wider acceptability than the current system, due to what he calls it "individualization." The current system, he argues, is politically acceptable because people think of themselves paying contributions to it and getting back benefits when they retire based upon *their* contributions. It is not a welfare system; it is system of forced savings in the minds of most people.

But Buchanan is worried that increasingly people will find this rationale unacceptable—given the current divergence between individuals' contributions and the amount that is paid back. He argues that future generations will be less and less certain that they're going to get their money's worth; they may lose faith in the system. The advantage of Buchanan's plan is that the individual gets his own piece of paper with a guaranteed rate of return. He argues that this is a much stronger guarantee than the *implicit* promise of benefits to be paid that every individual has as a member of the current system.

Buchanan argues that his proposed program also insulates social security from political interference and from *excessive and inequitable* spending on the part of Congress. Congress would not be able to manipulate the system so easily, taking some from one group in the population and giving more to other groups. Instead, a straight one-to-one relationship would exist on an individual basis—just as in private insurance.

Some critics of the Buchanan proposal argue, however, that it is very important for a government pension program to be able to redistribute income. Many people think that it is quite justifiable to redisstribute income through a social security program.

A more fundamental concern regarding the Buchanan proposal is that it calls for a radical change. The current program has strong support both from a broad segment of the population and within Congress. There is a question as to whether the Buchanan proposal would have any chance of getting accepted because it is so completely different and does not build on what we have at present. The tendency is for legislation to develop incrementally, and major changes that are proposed still have to embody in some way prior legislation.

Apart from the political feasibility of such a major change, it is questionable whether the resulting gain is worth the costs. The gains that are obtained in equity (by the reform) are obtained at a great cost. For example, there are major developmental, administrative, and information costs associated with a radical shift to a completely new program that has no established consumer acceptability or understanding.*

General Revenue Financing   Other people concerned about the financing of social security have also recommended the introduction of general governments revenues to help support the costs. Like Buchanan, many of them see the blanketing in of large groups of persons during the initial years as a burden that need not be financed by the payroll tax. Unlike Buchanan, however, most people call for general revenue financing without abandoning the basic structure of the current social security system.

General revenue financing was first suggested by the Committee on Economic Security, a presidential committee whose recommendations formed the basis of the original Social Security Act. The idea was also supported by the first Advisory Council on Social Security in 1937–38 and the one in 1947. Later advisory councils, however, did not see an immediate need for this additional source of financing or opposed general revenue financing as destructive of the insurance principles embodied in the program.

In 1944 Congress (over presidential veto) froze the payroll tax and authorized an appropriation from general revenue to the trust fund for "such additional sums as may be required to finance the benefits and payments under this title." Rather than representing an enthusiastic endorsement by Congress of the concept of general revenue financing, this action was more a byproduct of the division in Congress over when and how large social security reserves should grow. Ignoring the 1947 Advisory Council on Social Security's recommendation for a "government contribution," both the House Committee on Ways and Means and the Senate Finance Committee Reports in 1950 stated that the system "should be on a completely self-supporting basis," and Congress in that year repealed the general revenue provision.

Many who agree with the idea of general revenue financing favor restricting these payments to help meet the costs of "windfall benefits" (i.e., benefits given without contributions equal to the actuarial value of these benefits). In a "working paper" prepared for the U.S.

---

*See Browning (1973) for a discussion of income-distribution problems associated with the Buchanan plan and a proposed alternative.

Senate Special Committee on Aging, Nelson H. Cruikshank, president of the National Council of Senior Citizens, presented such a proposal:

> Workers already close to retirement age when the [social security] system was first started, or when coverage was extended to their employment, received full benefits even though the contributions they and their employers paid would finance only a small part of the benefit. While this was sound public policy and kept many old people off relief, it did mean that these benefits had to be financed from future contributions. There is no justification for expecting presently covered workers to pay for this "accrued liability"—estimated in the long run to amount to one-third of the total cost of the program—through a regressive payroll tax. A far fairer method would to be finance this share from general revenue sources to which all taxpayers contribute and through a more progressive tax structure. (U.S. Senate Special Committee on Aging, 1970)

A variety of arguments have been raised against general revenue financing. The major ones are:

1. That it would encourage excessive increases in benefits.
2. That it tends to integrate social security into the annual budget-review process and make social security more "political."
3. That it is contrary to the insurance and contributory principles of the program, which promote the political acceptability of social security.
4. That it would turn social security into a welfare program, with an associated congressional and public decline in support.

Changing the Payroll Tax Structure   A variety of proposals have been made to change the payroll tax. The principal approach suggested is to make the payroll tax rate progressive. One way this could be done is to provide individual lump-sum exemptions to the tax in the same way as exists in the current income tax law. Walter Reuther, for example, proposed in 1967 a $600 exemption per earner. Other proposals would allow exemptions for dependents, and some propose a "standard deduction" amount equal to that in the federal income tax law.

Alternatively, it has been proposed that the payroll tax be integrated with the income tax. The present tax withholdings for both social security and income taxes would continue, but at the end of the year the total amounts collected would be added together and applied to satisfying the individual's or couple's income tax liability. An excess of taxes over liability would be the basis for a tax refund. To accomplish this would require higher taxes.

Arguments against the above two proposals are similar to the ones raised against general revenue financing, but another type of reform proposal actually became law in 1975.

The 1975 Tax Act contained a one-year provision known as the "earned income credit" or "work bonus" for low-income workers *with children*. Under this provision, an eligible individual is allowed a tax credit equal to 10 percent of earned income up to $4000 a year (a rough approximation of his or her combined payroll tax). The tax credit is reduced (till it reaches zero at income levels of $8000) by 10 percent of "adjusted gross income" (or, if greater, the earned income) that exceeds $4000 per year.

The major justification for the amendment was to remove the work-disincentive effect of social security taxes on low-income workers. If the 1975 credit were made a permanent provision of the tax law and extended to people without children, it would offset most of the total payroll taxes paid on earnings of $4000 or less.

Again, some of the opposition to the work bonus amendment was based on its welfare character. Senator Sam J. Ervin, for example, charged in one floor debate over the credit that "it is robbery to take social security money and use it for welfare purposes." In addition, the Nixon Administration came out against an early version of the work bonus, arguing that the provision would create serious administrative problems and that it would complicate the development of sound income-maintenance policy by "adding yet another program to the many present assistance programs." The Ford Administration, using similar arguments, also argued against the provision.

Financing State and Local and Private Pensions

No less important are the issues that arise in connection with other types of pension plans. While social security in the United States operates without accumulating any significant reserves, we find that the reserves of other pension plans have increased dramatically in the past few decades (see Table 19). The federal civil service retirement system is the major exception—being financed, like social security, on the pay-as-you-go principle. Let us first look at private pensions and then the state and local government plans.

Private Pension Financing   In 1963 the Studebaker Corporation, a small producer of automobiles, went out of business. The company had established fourteen years before a pension plan that ultimately covered about 11,000 employees. When the company closed its South Bend, Indiana, plant, there were assets worth $24 million in the pension fund. But these assets were insufficient to meet all the "pension

Table 19   Pension Plan Assets, 1960–1973

Type	1960	1962	1965	1970	1973
			(Billions)		
Private	$51.9	$63.5	$86.5	$138.2	$179.0
Insured	$18.8	$21.6	$27.3	$ 41.2	$ 54.6
Noninsured	$33.1	$41.9	$59.2	$ 97.0	$124.4
State and Local	$19.6	$24.5	$33.1	$ 58.0	$ 80.2

Source: U.S. Securities and Exchange Commission, *Statistical Bulletin* (various years).

rights" that had been accumulated. The result: about 4500 workers got an average of only $600 apiece or 15 percent of the value of their rights. And those workers who had accumulated years of service but had not achieved pension vesting status got nothing.

Because of the number of workers affected and the prominence of the industry, the Studebaker case immediately became a favorite example to be used by those persons calling for private pension reform. Studebaker, and dozens of others, illustrate the major goal *and also the major hazard* of private pension financing—to insure that there are adequate funds so that promised benefits are, in fact, paid.

Prior to the 1974 pension reform legislation, most private plans financed pensions on a reserve basis, with a few operating on a partial or full pay-as-you-go basis. Now all plans covered by the 1974 act are required to meet its minimum funding standards.

In reviewing financing practices it is useful to group plans into three categories: (a) noninsured or trusteed plans, (b) insured plans, and (c) multi-employer plans. The majority of plans are noninsured or trusteed plans whose reserves are either self-administered by the individual company or administered by a trustee, in most cases commercial banks. Significantly, the great bulk of these reserves are administered by only about twenty-five banks! Insured plans are administered by various insurance companies. Multi-employer funds, usually the result of union collective bargaining, are often run by the unions themselves.

Less than a quarter of private plans require a contribution to the plan by employees; the rest are financed entirely by the employer. A major reason for the prevalence of "noncontributory" plans is the fact that employee contributions from earnings are subject, with certain exceptions, to federal income taxes. In contrast, the money employers put into a pension fund is not subject to any taxes. In addition, employee contributions greatly complicate the administration of a plan—requiring the establishment of a pension account for each worker and policies regulating these accounts. And, as we indicated in Chapter 7, noncontributory plans usually reduce employer pension costs during the earning years.

Although most firms have established reserve funds to be built up over the years as their pension liabilities grow, many of the pension rights granted under the plans remain in jeopardy as a result of "past service credits." When new plans are established or old plans liberalized, the usual practice is to give workers full pension credits for their years of work prior to the plan's establishment or liberalization. While the pension liabilities for these past service credits accrue immediately, employers usually adopt a payment schedule for funding these liabilities that, in the past, extended over a 10- to 40-year period (and sometimes longer). As long as this unfunded liability remains, a plan that terminates will be unable to pay its promised future pension benefits. This is what happened in the Studebaker case. And, in fact, many plans have terminated over the years—with a resultant loss of pension rights to thousands of workers.

A study by Frank Griffin and Charles L. Trowbridge (1969) of funding status indicated that "the level of funding achieved by 1966 within the private pension movement as a whole [was] higher than we might expect." (Trowbridge, 1970) As might be expected, they found that the longer a plan had been in existence, the higher the level of funding. Plans in existence for 15 or more years had assets, on average, sufficient to cover about 95 percent of all accrued benefits. And more than half of all plans studied were fully funded.

Many plans, however, still have sizable unfunded liabilities. For example, one large American automobile manufacturer had an unfunded pension liability of $86 million when it initiated a retirement plan in 1950. Yet a company official reported that the unfunded past service cost *had grown* to $870 million by the end of 1967—over ten times the initial unfunded amount—as a result of continuing plan liberalization. Moreover, Griffin and Trowbridge found in their study that about one-third of the 10-year or younger plans has unfunded liabilities of 40 percent or more.

The 1974 pension reform legislation requires that all new plans must fund past service liabilities in no more than 30 years; plans in existence prior to the 1975 law have 40 years. Perhaps a more significant aspect of the law is the establishment of an insurance program to protect employees against the loss of vested benefits in the event of plan termination.

A new Pension Benefit Guaranty Corporation is in charge of this program. All covered plans must pay into the insurance fund. In addition, the corporation has authority to borrow up to $100 million from the federal treasury. The resulting insurance program represents a major step forward in providing workers covered by private pension significant protection from the potential financing problems connected with plan termination.

State and Local Pension Financing   Pension plans established to provide retirement benefits for state and local government employees are *not* covered by any provisions of the Employee Retirement Income Security Act of 1974. Substantial political pressure from various groups in the states caused the drafters of the legislation to exempt these plans—lest the resulting opposition to the bill endanger its chances of passage. The minimum funding provisions of the bill, which would have necessitated sizable tax increases in many states, were in large part responsible for the opposition. No doubt opposition was also based on the tradition of state autonomy in the pension area and the fears of many government employees that compliance under the proposed law would be costly and ultimately result in their receiving smaller pensions.

There are over 2000 state and local government pension plans. Unlike private pensions, state and local plans almost always require a contribution from the employee that is some percent of salary. Most state and local plans are funded. The amount of funding varies greatly among the various plans but usually does not approach the extent of funding achieved by private plans.

Unfortunately, data on the actuarial status of the thousands of government plans (or even a representational sample of them) are not available. A study by James A. Maxwell (1975) of the pension plans in the twenty-nine largest cities "shows that many of them are in trouble." Using the ratio of current payments to assets as a rough indication of the financial strength or weakness of a fund, Maxwell also identifies four states where plan financing is weak: Delaware, Massachusetts, West Virginia, and Maine.

Tilove's assessment of the current situation is that significant improvements have occurred in the funding situation of state and local plans but that funding is in fact poorest where it is most needed:

> The cases most in need of attention are the systems of the financially distressed urban centers and of the many smaller cities and counties that have no real assurance of future ability to pay. It is their fiscal difficulties that have kept many on pay-as-you-go, and that is precisely why they should begin to fund on an actuarial basis—so that they may

confront the long-term implications of their pension decisions and, by the same policy, assure the ultimate security of their employees. (Tilove, 1976)

In many ways, state and local pension financing falls in between social security financing and private pension plans. Like the federal government, state and city governments are not likely ever to cease operations, and pensions are protected by law and the taxing powers of the government. But, like private business, state and cities are not assured of a continually growing financing base. Some states and cities may experience a net loss of businesses or population and/or their tax base. These shifts are difficult to predict and can cause serious problems if pension costs (based on past promises) are rising while the government's tax revenues are growing very slowly or falling.

Because pension benefits can be liberalized without any substantial increases in current costs, some people fear that pension plans will be liberalized without due regard to the future financing implications. It is argued that the political process is particularly susceptible to this problem because the conduct of state and local politicians is often "determined by relatively short-run considerations. The impact of failing to adhere to actuarial principles will frequently fall upon a different mayor and a different city council. In these circumstances, concessions that condemn a city to future impoverishment may not seem intolerable." (Wellington and Winter, 1971) Despite the large number of state and local funds, the magnitude of fund assets, the growth of benefit levels, and the fears of many professionals regarding state and local pension financing, very little attention has been given to the impact of these plans on the economic status of the current and future aged. Individuals covered by these plans, and relying on them for retirement security, should be aware of this gap in our knowledge. And state and local taxpayers should probably be more sensitive to the long-term costs of these pensions and support an increase in the availability of information in this area.

Suggested Readings

The American Enterprise Institute. *Private Pensions and the Public Interest*. Washington, D.C. The American Enterprise Institute, 1970.
Proceedings of a conference that dealt extensively with private pension financing.
Brittain, John A. *The Payroll Tax for Social Security*. Washington, D.C.: The Brookings Institution, 1972.
An economic study of the payroll tax, the intergenerational equity question, and various reform proposals.

Feldstein, Martin. "Toward a Reform of Social Security." *The Public Interest* 40 (Summer 1975): 75-95.

Feldstein answers the "social security bankruptcy" arguments but warns that social security is reducing aggregate personal savings and may result in lower economic growth with resultant implications for pension equity.

Nader, Ralph, and Kate Blackwell. *You and Your Pension.* New York: Grossman, 1973.

A guide to the potential problems that might be encountered by persons covered by private pensions (written prior to the 1974 reform legislation). The book also reviews the many financing problems and policy issues.

Projector, Dorothy S. "Should the Payroll Tax Finance Higher Benefits Under OASDHI? A Review of the Issues." *Journal of Human Resources* 4 (Winter 1969): 60-75.

A somewhat dated but excellent discussion of some of the major issues.

Subcommittee on Fiscal Policy, U.S. Joint Economic Committee. *Issues in Financing Retirement Income.* Paper No. 18 in "Studies in Public Welfare." Washington, D.C.: U.S. Government Printing Office, 1974.

The best summary available of the financial history of social security and the issues as they have been discussed over the years. It also contains a comprehensive bibliography of congressional documents, monographs, and journal articles on social security financing.

Thompson, Lawrence H. *An Analysis of the Factors Currently Determining Benefit Level Adjustments in the Social Security Program.* Technical Analysis Paper No. 1. Office of Income Security Policy, Office of the Assistant Secretary of Planning and Evaluation. Washington, D.C.: Department of Health, Education, and Welfare, 1974.

An explanation of the overadjustment (double adjustment or "decoupling") problem arising from the social security indexing mechanism adopted in 1972.

U.S. Senate Special Committee on Aging. *Women and Social Security: Adapting to a New Era.* A working paper prepared by the Task Force on Women and Social Security. Washington, D.C.: U.S. Government Printing Office, 1975.

An excellent summary of the various issues, including a discussion of various proposed changes in women's benefits.

Chapter Nine

Prospects for
the Future

As we look to the future, we can anticipate continuing improvement in the economic situation of the elderly population. Most of the improvement of the past several decades is (and much of the future improvement will be) the result of better public and private pensions to help individuals carry out the retirement-preparation job. The last four chapters surveyed past pension developments and discussed some of the problems that remain to be resolved in the future. Despite the remaining problems, however, we can look forward to improvement in the general living standards of a large segment of the elderly population as a result of their participation in pension programs.

In addition to rising pension coverage and benefit levels, there are a number of other specific factors operating to improve the future economic status of the elderly. First, there is the "demographic turnover" in the aged population. Every day approximately 4000 Americans celebrate their sixty-fifth birthday and approximately 3000 persons over age 64 die. Those leaving the elderly population because of death are usually older and in the poorest financial situation, while many of the new aged start this period of life with pension incomes that were undreamed of not many years ago. Quickly disappearing is the "no pension generation"—workers too old to achieve regular pension status when social security or their employers' pension plans were initially established.

A second factor is the existence of a better welfare program for the aged—with higher benefit levels and better inflation protection. The Supplemental Security Income program—together with state supplementation—was launched in 1974. (See Chapter 6) It will take a few years to work out some of the problems connected with establishing this new program, but we can expect that gradually more people who are eligible will learn about and take advantage of the program and that most of the initial administrative delays in the payment of benefits will be eliminated.

Welfare expenditures have never been politically popular among legislators. Yet there have been some indications in recent years of a more favorable attitude developing in the United States toward government action to eliminate poverty. This more favorable attitude seems to hold especially for the elderly. Certainly, as the nation's wealth grows over time, we find ourselves collectively better able to afford the expenditures needed to raise the incomes of the poor. Therefore, we can anticipate additional real increases in welfare benefits for the aged.

Third, as the long-run rise of 1 or 2 percent annually in real incomes of American families continues, there will be a greater potential for individual saving out of that income. While historically the data show (see Table 16, page 76) that few families have been able or willing to save much (beyond the equity in a home), we can probably expect some incremental improvements in this area.

Problems Remaining

Despite the substantial gains that have been achieved, there are some major economic problems likely to remain with us for many years to come.

Table 20   Percent of Men and Women in Poverty, 1973

Age	Men	Women
Total Age 16 or Older	7.4	11.6
16–21 years	10.4	13.2
Family Head	13.2	75.6
Other Family Member	8.3	9.3
Unrelated Individual	38.1	49.6
22–64 years	5.8	9.7
Family Head	4.6	33.4
Other Family Member	5.7	5.2
Unrelated Individual	15.2	22.8
65 or Older	12.4	19.0
Family Head	9.5	16.8
Other Family Member	8.0	8.0
Unrelated Individual	27.1	33.5

Source: U.S. Bureau of the Census, *Characteristics of the Low-Income Population: 1973,* Current Population Reports Series P-60, No. 98. (Washington, D.C.: U.S. Government Printing Office, 1975).

Poverty among Elderly Women Perhaps most significant in the trend of poverty among the aged is the economic situation of aged women, especially widows. Poverty analyst Mollie Orshansky (1974) writes that "in our society, at every age and every stage, women are more vulnerable to poverty than men, especially if they must do double duty as both family head and homemaker." Table 20 shows the separate poverty rates for men and women in 1973. In almost every category the rates for women are higher, often higher by a wide margin. Focusing on *aged* women in poverty, Table 21 shows that the largest number of such women are widowed (about 1½ million) and that the group with the highest incidence of poverty is "separated women" (55 percent). Fortunately, increased welfare benefits through the Supplemental Security Income program are helping to improve the incomes of these very low-income women.

Table 21 Aged Women with Poverty Level Incomes, 1973

Marital Status	Below Poverty Level	
	Number[a]	Percent
Married, Husband Present	375	8.3
Married, Husband Absent	29	*[b]
Widowed	1578	24.9
Divorced	97	31.4
Separated	55	54.5
Never Married	165	21.6

Source: U.S. Bureau of the Census, *Characteristics of the Low-Income Population: 1973*, Current Population Reports Series P-60, No. 98. (Washington, D.C.: U.S. Government Printing Office, 1975).
[a]Thousands.
[b]Base less than 75,000.

A different problem exists for *nonpoor* women who have not achieved their own pension eligibility. Existing public and private pension programs typically reduce or stop pension benefits when "the worker" dies. In the case of social security, the benefit drops by one-third. Private pension practices vary widely—with widow benefits being very low and usually an elective feature of the plan. As a result, widows of workers eligible for private pensions usually do not receive any pension. A staff report of the U.S. Commission on Civil Rights recently reported that only 2 percent of the elderly widows of employees who were covered by private pensions are currently receiving benefits.

Women as workers also face many special problems that affect their ability to qualify for large pension benefits in their own right. Lower earnings and intermittent work histories are not uncommon among women. These two factors result in lower social security pensions (or in not qualifying for benefits at all).

Private pension coverage for women is lower than for men; in 1972 only 36 percent of full-time working women were covered, as compared to 52 percent for men. Vesting requirements of 10–15 years penalize women who move in and out of the labor force.

Until recently relatively little attention was given to the economic status of women and their changing roles. Likewise, research to understand the changes in the economic situation of women in old age has been minimal. Both areas are now receiving quite a lot of attention. (*See* Kahne, 1975) Moreover, changes in social security are under study, and there is evidence that many private pensions are improving those provisions that are important to women. How quickly the problems in this area will be solved, however, is still very unclear.

The Nonsteady Worker Just as women are at a relative disadvantage in accumulating pension rights because of intermittent labor-force participation, there are both men and women who cannot achieve "good pensions" because of nonsteady employment. A significant number of workers are faced with one or more of the following problems that interfere with employment:

1. Health problems, ranging from total and complete disability to specific impairments that interfere with particular job functions.
2. Job discrimination.
3. Plant closedowns, which force older workers with experience, seniority, and special skills to compete for alternative opportunities.
4. Skill obsolescence, causing loss of jobs in declining industrial sectors and/or long-term unemployment due to the lack of demand for obsolete skills.
5. Recessional periods, when marginal workers are unable to find suitable employment.

As a result of problems such as these, some workers arrive at the retirement period with an intermittent employment record. When their gaps in employment are in the later years, these years of *potentially highest* earnings are lost for pension computation purposes.

Unemployable older workers usually "retire" at the first opportunity—taking early retirement benefits at significantly reduced levels from those available at the regular retirement age. A 1969 survey by the

Social Security Administration, for example, found that almost half of the men claiming social security benefits at age 62 had no private pension and did not want to retire when they had to leave their job. As Lenore E. Bixby (1970) has observed, "it appears. . . that the early retirement provisions of the OASDHI program often function as an intermediate disability program, providing benefits for older disabled workers who are unable to meet the eligibility requirements for disability insurance, are waiting to have a disability determination completed, or choose not to apply for disability benefits."

The circumstances faced by workers vary tremendously, however; some have few or no problems and some have very serious difficulties. The question that arises is whether present policies and programs are adequate to deal with these differences. Various proposals have been made for improving unemployment, disability, and retraining programs. Before programmatic changes can be made, however, certain policy questions must be dealt with.

First, there is the question of whether the burden and solution to problems generated during the period prior to retirement are to be primarily the responsibility of the individual. If so, actuarially reduced private and public pensions are examples of program development that give the individual flexibility in deciding when the pension should start but do not add to program costs. That is, persons forced into early retirement by certain problems can collect a reduced pension, but if they want to maintain their income at a higher level, they must do so through supplemental income sources.

Alternatively, if it is decided to develop a national policy to better assist workers with special problems, should the policy be to maintain the income level for the affected families at or close to their prior living standard or should the policy simply guarantee that a family should not fall below a designated minimum?

What should be the basic mechanism for any public program in this area—an insurance-type program, a welfare program, or what? Several countries in Europe have established a variety of special mechanisms for assisting older workers who have employment problems but are too young to receive regular pensions. West Germany, for example, permits older workers with long-term unemployment to qualify for retirement pensions before the regular retirement age.

In the United States, there are a number of programs to help workers with employment problems. These include disability insurance, Workmen's Compensation, the Vocational Rehabilitation Program, and the Comprehensive Employment and Training Act. In addition, there are some special programs for older workers: (a) the Age Discrimination in

Employment Act, (b) special programs (VISTA, SCORE, RSVP, and Foster Grandparent) under The Domestic Volunteer Service Act, and (c) The Older Americans Community Service Employment Program.

All these programs in the United States are very limited in scope and fail to deal adequately with the magnitude and variety of the older-worker problems listed above. Remaining to be decided are two basic questions: how much more in this problem area does the nation desire to do and what mechanisms will be used?

Medical Costs Even with Medicare, the elderly have had to make sizable expenditures for health care. Medicare, however, has helped to regularize and level off these expenditures, while removing much of the insecurity caused by large medical bills arising from "medium-term" illness.

Figure 11 shows what percentage of various types of health care expenditures were paid for by Medicare over the 1967–74 period. In 1974, for example, over 60 percent of hospital care and over 50 percent of physicians' services were covered. In contrast, the fact that only about 3 percent of nursing-home-care expenses were paid for by Medicare illustrates a major problem. Major gaps still exist in health-care economic security.

The two problems most often cited are the dangers of progressive impoverishment and the financial drain of expenses not covered by health insurance. The former problem usually results when an illness extends over a very long period of time or the person's state of health requires nonhospital institutionalization. Medicare provides benefits for inpatient hospital services up to 90 days in each benefit period* and up to 60 consecutive days in a skilled nursing facility. Care in a posthospital care service or convalescent section of a hospital is available up to 100 days but qualification for these benefits is difficult because of stringent rules of eligibility. Nursing-home care is authorized under Medicare but only in very limited circumstances.

All these limits on insurance protection are a problem for older people. "The fear of a long and costly final illness haunts many old people. To end one's life as a ward of the state, or to drain the resources of one's children, is an all-too-frequent prospect for old persons in America." (Brown, 1972)

When Medicare coverage runs out older persons must either have supplemental private coverage or finance the health costs them-

*A benefit period begins when the individual is admitted to a hospital and when he has not received inpatient hospital or skilled nursing facility services for 60 consecutive days. After the 90 days are exhausted, each person has a lifetime reserve of 60 days of hospital care for his optional use at a shared cost.

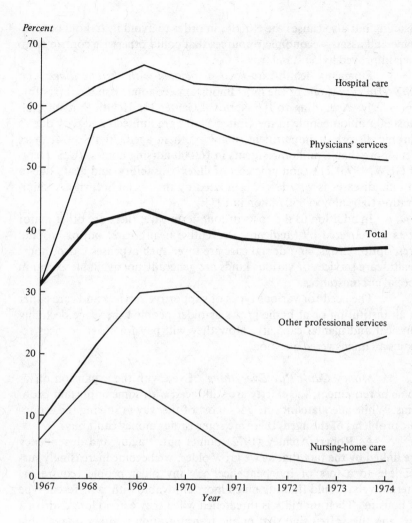

Figure 11. Percent of Aged[a] Personal Health Care Expenditures Paid by Medicare, 1967-74[b]

Source: Errata to Marjorie Smith Mueller and Robert M. Gibson, "Age Differences in Health Care Spending, Fiscal Year 1974," *Social Security Bulletin* 38 (June 1975): 3–16.
[a]Persons aged 65 and over.
[b]Fiscal years.

selves. Once they draw down their assets sufficiently, they may become eligible for means-tested Medic*aid* benefits, whose eligibility requirements vary from state to state. This pauperization process is not only demeaning but also causes the elderly, in order to avoid it, to hold onto income and assets—economic resources that could otherwise contribute to their improved living standards.

Financing health-care costs *associated with chronic illness and long-term care* is one of the most important economic issues confronting the elderly. According to the National Center for Health Statistics, almost 30 million people in the United States are limited in activity due to chronic disease or impairment, many of them aged. In 1973–74, there were more than a million residents in 16,000 nursing homes. (U.S. Dept. of HEW, 1975) The economic cost of illness, disability, and death due to chronic diseases is very large, estimated by the Social Security Administration to be almost $50 billion in 1974.

In addition to the costs of long-term care, there are other major costs not covered by Medicare. Preventive health care, out-of-hospital prescription drugs, and dental care are three such expenses. Also, home health-care services of various kinds are generally not available except in special circumstances.

The need for various types of supportive services and care either in an institution or at home grows as older people experience declining physical and mental capacity. How they will pay for these services remains an unanswered question.

Money Can't Buy Everything   Even with the expansion of income in retirement, the elderly are still faced with some important problems. While adequate income goes most of the way in solving the economic problems of the aged, there are some things money can't buy.

As Robert Atchley (1972) points out, "aging and dependency are linked by the fact that as we grow older, we become increasingly susceptible to a loss of independence." Many older people require or, alternatively, would find life much more enjoyable with, a different type of housing. Their mobility is threatened when they can no longer drive a car, and they often find that public transportation is either unavailable or inadequate. Illness and disability often make the ordinary tasks of dressing, eating, and shopping a major problem.

In Senate testimony, Dr. Wilma Donahue, Director of the International Center for Social Gerontology, discussed one of the unmet special needs that arises as people grow older:

> Senator Williams, my purpose in appearing before your subcommittee this morning is to support the position of the Congress and of increasing numbers of researchers and practitioners in the field of aging that the time, knowledge, and resources are at hand to fill a glaring gap in the continuum of housing that the United States should be making available to its older population. Specifically, it has been amply

demonstrated that there is need for specially designed housing with a variety of associated services ["congregate housing"]* for scores, if not hundreds, of thousands of older people who must now live under growing apprehension of having too soon to seek refuge in long-term medical care facilities as they progress through the later years of their lives. These are the impaired but not ill, noninstitutionalized, often low-income older people who must struggle against rising odds to maintain themselves in the community. (U.S. Subcommittee on Housing for the Elderly, 1975)

Increasing attention is currently being given to the various services required or desired by the elderly that are either not offered in the marketplace or not offered in sufficient quantity and quality. One of the major goals of the U.S. Administration on Aging, for example, is to promote comprehensive coordinated services for older persons. But action in this area is still very experimental; programs are widely scattered and unavailable to most of the aged. It will be many years before we know exactly what are the best services to offer, how these services should be provided, and what mechanisms should be used to finance them.

Private Pension Weaknesses   As we indicated in Chapter 7, private pensions are relatively young and still evolving. It is appropriate to repeat three major problems that have not yet been resolved. First, there is the problem of inflation; as yet no completely satisfactory way of adjusting private pensions in retirement for increases in living costs has been found. Second, there is the problem of vesting; current vesting practices (a) still result in pension losses for those workers changing jobs relatively frequently, and (b) do not adjust the benefit rights of "vested" job-changers for inflation.

The third and probably most important problem is incomplete coverage. Currently only about 45 percent of wage and salary workers in private industry are covered by private pensions. The result is that many people reaching retirement age must rely solely on social security pensions. Figure 12 illustrates the pension disparity among men retiring in early 1970. This figure shows the proportion of retirees with less and more than 50 percent replacement of total earnings.

In Figure 12 the "social security only" recipients are divided into two groups: those with earnings—in their 3 years of highest earnings during the last 10—below the social security taxable-earnings base and those with earnings above the maximum in 1 or all of the 3 highest years.

*Congregate housing is defined by Dr. Donahue as "a residential environment which incorporates shelter and services, needed by the functionally impaired and socially deprived but not ill elderly to enable them to maintain or return to a semi-independent life-style and avoid institutionalization as they grow older."

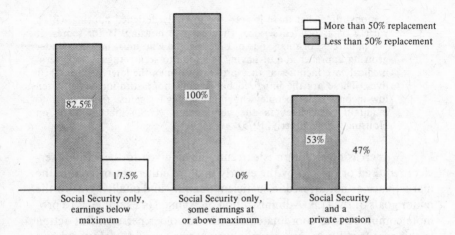

Figure 12. Proportion of Male Social Security Retirees with Less and More Than 50 Percent Earnings Replacement, Early 1970.
Source: Social Security Administration.

The third group is retirees with dual pension coverage, receiving *both* social security and a private pension.

    While a relatively high proportion (45 percent) of retirees with dual pension coverage received pensions replacing more than 50 percent of preretirement earnings, *most men receiving only social security received less than 50 percent replacement.*

    We have improved public and private pensions significantly. But if present trends continue, the retirement-income disparity created by our present dual pension system will grow larger and could create serious social tension between the resulting "pension elite" covered by two pensions and those less fortunate.

    The current tax incentive to promote private retirement savings is seen by some as a partial solution to the coverage problem. In a message to Congress on December 8, 1971, President Nixon first proposed that pension legislation be enacted that would contain saving incentives. This proposal was embodied in bills introduced in the House by Representatives Wilbur Mills and John W. Byrnes and in the Senate by Senator Carl Curtis. The legislation was enacted as part of the private pension-reform legislation that became law in September 1974.

    President Nixon's proposal, and the subsequent law, permits wage and salary earners to set up their own individual retirement plans (IRA's) if they are not covered by any qualified pension plan. Employees not covered by private pension plans can deduct up to 15 percent of earned income (up to $1500 a year) to be set aside free of taxation until subsequently paid out. In addition, the 1974 pension-reform legislation liberalized existing limitations on contributions to retirement plans for the self-employed (generally called Keogh or HR 10 plans). The self-employed are now allowed to deduct 15 percent of earned income up to $7500 (instead of 10 percent up to $2500 under previous law).

In proposing the legislation, President Nixon argued that it would encourage people to save and that public policy should reward and reinforce this type of activity. In transmitting the legislation, he said:

> Self-reliance, prudence, and independence are qualities which our government should work to encourage among our people. These are also the qualities which are involved when a person chooses to invest in a retirement savings plan, setting aside money today so that he will have greater security tomorrow. In this respect pension plans are a direct expression of some of the finest elements in the American character. Public policy should be designed to reward and reinforce these qualities.

The President also argued that this legislation would be responsive to the inequity that existed between those people who were covered by private pensions and those who were not. People covered by private pensions receive favorable tax treatment because contributions made by the employer on their behalf are not taxable. These private pension contributions are only taxable at the time they are paid out, usually at much lower tax rates because retirement-income levels are reduced over prior work periods.

These were the two principal reasons given by the President in favor of such legislation. Other people have argued that by encouraging people to save for retirement individually, one allows them to control their own investments and decide what they want to invest in and the amount of risk they want to take. If you are a member of a private pension plan you have nothing to say about the investment policy of the plan. Often the gains of good investment accrue only to the employer. If you are a sophisticated person with regard to financial matters and economics, you might be able to do better with the same amount of funds, especially if you are willing to take some risks.

And finally, it has been argued that this approach is an alternative to increasing and expanding the social welfare programs that currently exist to help older people. Such tax incentives, it is argued, give people the option to build upon their social security base and give them the freedom to choose how to do it.

A major objection to the "incentive for saving" tax plan is that it provides greater benefits to workers with higher earnings. Higher-earnings workers will be able to set aside a larger absolute amount of income; 15 percent of $6000, for example, is not as much as 15 percent of $10,000 ($900 versus $1500). Moreover, if you are a higher-income person you are more likely to be financially able to save up to the maximum and get the maximum tax deduction.

But more importantly, the proportion of lower-paid workers who will take advantage of this opportunity for tax-sheltered saving is likely to be smaller than in the case of more highly paid persons. The fear that such tax-exemption proposals would turn into tax loopholes for higher-income people was the principal argument voiced in Congress against the legislation when it was proposed.

In this regard, the experience of a similar tax-incentive plan in Canada lends insight. The Canadian government introduced "registered retirement savings plans" in 1957. Workers not covered by a private pension, persons in non-contributory plans, and employees whose own pension contributions are below a certain amount are eligible to participate.

Robert N. Schoeplein (1966) found in a study he made in 1962 of the Canadian plan (after it had been in operation a few years) that very few people were participating. Those who did were concentrated in the higher-income groups.

A more recent study of the Canadian experience provides data on participation for 1973. Table 22 shows the proportion of persons filing tax returns who contributed to the special savings plans. While only 7 percent of all tax filers participated during 1973, about one-third to one-half of the filers with incomes exceeding $15,000 made contributions to the tax-exempt plans. Other tabulations (not shown in Table 22) indicate wide variation in participation by occupation. As might be expected, participation is highest in occupations with large amounts of self-employment. For example, 56 percent of filing accountants, medical doctors, dentists, and lawyers participated in such plans. In contrast, however, less than 10 percent of the farmers filing tax returns were contributors.

How well does the Canadian Registered Retirement Savings Plan (RRSP) program fill the retirement-preparation gap for those workers not covered by private pensions? About 64 percent of the entire Canadian labor force is *not* covered by private pensions. If we subtract from this noncovered group those workers who participated in RRSP during 1973, the "uncovered" group changes very little, from about 64 percent to 59 percent of the labor force.*

*Based upon unpublished statistics provided by Harry Weitz, Chief, Pension Section, Statistics Canada.

Table 22   Contributors to Canadian Registered Retirement Savings Plans

Income Class	Percent of Tax Filers		
	Men	Women	Total
Under $2000	.2	.1	.2
$2000–2999	.6	.5	.6
$3000–3999	1.0	1.1	1.0
$4000–4999	1.9	2.0	1.9
$5000–5999	2.5	3.3	2.9
$6000–6999	3.9	5.7	4.6
$7000–7999	5.1	7.5	5.8
$8000–8999	6.4	10.4	7.4
$9000–9999	7.7	13.7	8.7
$10,000–14,999	12.6	21.2	13.5
$15,000–19,999	26.7	33.8	27.2
$20,000–24,999	40.6	34.6	40.2
$25,000 and Over	56.7	26.3	54.6
Total	8.8	3.7	6.9

Source: Revenue Canada Taxation and Statistics Canada.

The experience of Canada seems to confirm that tax-exempt savings programs tend to be used more by higher-income groups. An alternative approach to the private pension coverage problem is to require all employers to provide pension or require uncovered workers to join a government-run supplemental program. This approach is currently being developed in Great Britain and Switzerland, for example.

Alternatively, the United States could rely more heavily on social security for the bulk of pension income. Benefit levels could be raised, reducing the necessity of major reliance on private pensions. This is the approach currently used in West Germany, Belgium, and Sweden (to name only a few countries). Private pensions exist in all these countries, but they are clearly supplemental to social security covering almost all workers.

Will We Pay the Price of Economic Adequacy?

Providing adequately for the retirement period is an expensive proposition. As the retirement age declines, we face the prospect of providing individuals with income and services for a 20–30 year period outside the labor force. Increasingly, people are developing expectations that retirement can and should be an enjoyable period of life and that economic resources should be sufficient to avoid the limitations imposed on retirement living by financial stringency. Unfortunately, if individuals begin to worry and seriously plan for their own retirement shortly before retirement, the magnitude of the financing problem becomes insuperable for most. The best and easiest way of accumulating the resources necessary for retirement is to begin very early. But historically most people have shown a reluctance to think about retirement until it is *almost* a reality or until it *is* a reality. The result has been a great deal of poverty among the aged.

Pension systems and, before them, families have stepped in to provide needed economic support for many of these people—often preventing destitution. But the level of support was often very low. Yet (as we discussed in Chapter 8) the financial burden imposed on the working population, even at these low levels of support, has created political concern. And, as we indicated, there is particular concern regarding the future burden.

What are the prospects for getting people to agree to finance higher levels of support? It seems to me that one of the best answers is provided by the individuals *now covered* by good private pensions and social security. The combined reduction in their take-home pay to provide social security and a good private pension is quite large (about 16–20 percent). Yet there is little complaining from this group, probably in large part because these costs are taken out before they ever get their earnings check.

Likewise, we can look at the European experience. Other industrialized countries have payroll taxes that range between 16 and 20 percent. Again, we see very little political opposition in these countries to this level of taxation for pension purposes.

In 1961, then Secretary of Health, Education, and Welfare Abraham Ribicoff stated that he thought the limit to public acceptance of the social security payroll tax was 10 percent. We have passed through that ceiling without difficulty. Now people worry about the high rates in the year 2010 or 2020. But as economist Martin Feldstein (1975) has pointed out:

> An increase in the social security tax rate to 16 or 20 percent would be a substantial increase.... There are some who believe that such high rates would create an intolerable burden on low-income and middle-income families. This is a false argument that ignores the substantial increase in real earnings that these families will enjoy at the same time that tax rates rise. Even a tax rate increase of 10 percentage points over the next 50 years is only an increase of 0.2 percent per year. The higher tax would absorb only one tenth of the annual real wage growth of two percent. Stated somewhat differently, with a two percent annual rate of

growth, real wages would rise by 200 percent between now and 2030, and the higher social security tax would absorb no more than 10 percentage points of this 200 percentage point increase in real wages.

Thus, it is important to remember the political acceptability of gradual increases in tax rates. This suggests that better pensions should be phased in over a period of years—similar to the way many other countries have introduced the major improvements in their programs. And it is probably wise to anticipate the demographic bulge and consequent sharp rise in costs beginning around the year 2010 as a result of the World War II "baby boom."

Also, there is a need for a greater awareness of the intra- and intergenerational equity issues. As the costs of aged retirement living increase, more attention should be given to these issues in order both to maintain public confidence in and support for the programs and to use with maximum effectiveness the money allocated.

The major economic issue is not whether—in the face of other public expenditure needs such as urban blight, national defense, and pollution—we can have better pensions and services for the aged. Rather, the issue is better posed as whether we want a higher standard of living in our retirement years at the expense of a lower standard in our younger years.

Suggested Readings

Browning, Edgar K. *Redistribution and the Welfare System.* Washington, D.C.: The American Enterprise Institute, 1975.
Browning argues that the present system of welfare transferred nearly $80 billion (cash and in-kind) to the poorest fourth of the American population in 1973 and that there has been a significant improvement in the relative status of the low-income population that is not reflected in official statistics because in-kind income is not counted. While data for the aged are not presented, the general argument has important implications for evaluating the economic status of the low-income aged.
Hudson, Robert B., and Robert H. Binstock. "Political Systems and Aging." In Robert H. Binstock and Ethel Shanas, eds. *The Handbook of Aging and the Social Sciences.* New York: Van Nostrand Reinhold, 1976.
A survey of what we know about the political attitudes and behavior of aging persons. The chapter has an excellent discussion of "aging power" and aging organizations, with insightful analysis of the political realities involved in improving the social and economic status of the elderly through government action.

Neugarten, Bernice L., ed. "Aging in the Year 2000: A Look at the Future." *The Gerontologist* 15, No. 1, Part II (February 1975): 3–40.
Preliminary findings are reported from a project investigating various changes occurring in the aging milieu.

Rejda, George E., and Richard J. Shepler. "The Impact of Zero Population Growth on the OASDHI Program." *The Journal of Risk and Insurance* 40 (September 1973): 313–325.
Using projections of the U.S. Census Bureau, the authors assess the likely impact of zero population growth on social security financing. They argue that there is a need for general revenue financing.

Subcommittee on Aging of the Senate Committee on Labor and Public Welfare and U.S. Senate Special Committee on Aging. *Post-White House Conference on Aging Reports, 1973*. Washington, D.C.: U.S. Government Printing Office, 1973.
The recommendations of the White House Conference, the reaction to or action taken by the Nixon Administration to the recommendations, and an analysis prepared by study panels of the Post-Conference Board of the White House Conference on Aging.

U.S. Senate Special Committee on Aging. *Future Directions in Social Security*. Parts 1–11. Washington, D.C.: U.S. Government Printing Office, 1974, 1975.
A series of hearings held by the committee during 1973–76, exploring various aspects of social security and seeking to develop information on recommended changes.

References

Aaron, Henry J.; John A. Brittain; Joseph A. Pechman; Alice Rivlin; Charles Schultze; and Nancy H. Teeters. 1972. *Washington Post* (October 4).

Advisory Council on Social Security. 1975. Reports. Washington, D.C.: mimeographed.

Atchley, Robert. 1972. *The Social Forces in Later Life*. Belmont, Calif.: Wadsworth.

Batten, Michael D. 1973. "Application of a Unique Industrial Health System." *Industrial Gerontology* (Fall): 38–48.

Bernstein, Merton. 1973. "Rehabilitating Workmen's Compensation: Alternatives for the Future." In Philip Booth, ed. *Social Security: Policy for the Seventies*. Ann Arbor: Institute of Labor and Industrial Relations, University of Michigan and Wayne State University, pp. 132–172.

Bixby, Lenore E. 1970. "Income of People Aged 65 and Over." *Social Security Bulletin* 33 (April): 3–34.

Bosworth, Barry; James S. Duesenberry; and Andrew S. Carron. 1975. *Capital Needs in the Seventies*. Washington, D.C.: The Brookings Institution.

Boulding, Kenneth. 1958. *Principles of Economic Policy*. Englewood Cliffs, N.J.: Prentice Hall.

Brittain, John A. 1972. *The Payroll Tax for Social Security*. Washington, D.C.: The Brookings Institution.

Brown, J. Douglas. 1972. *An American Philosophy of Social Security*. Princeton, N.J.: Princeton University Press.

_____. 1973. Memorandum. In U.S. Senate Special Committee on Aging. *Future Directions in Social Security*. Part 3. Washington, D.C.: U.S. Government Printing Office, pp. 220–221.

Browning, Edgar K. 1973. "Social Insurance and Intergenerational Transfers." *Journal of Law and Economics* (October): 215–237.

Buchanan, James M. 1968. "Social Insurance in a Growing Economy: A Proposal for Radical Reform." *National Tax Journal* (December): 386–395.

Cardwell, James B. 1975. Testimony. In U.S. Subcommittee on Social Security, Committee on Ways and Means. *Financing the Social Security System*. Washington, D.C.: U.S. Government Printing Office.

Caswell, Jerry. 1974. *Economic Efficiency in Pension Plan Administration: A Study of the Construction Industry.* Ph.D. dissertation, University of Pennsylvania.

Chen, Yung-Ping, and Kwang-Wen Chu. 1974. "Tax-benefit Ratios and Rates of Return Under OASI: 1974 Retirees and Entrants." *The Journal of Risk and Insurance* 41 (June): 189–206.

Cohen, Wilbur J. 1957. *Retirement Policies Under Social Security.* Berkeley: University of California Press.

Cohen, Wilbur J., and Milton Friedman. 1972. *Social Security: Universal or Selective?* Rational Debate Seminars. Washington, D.C.: American Enterprise Institute.

Cutler, Neal E., and Robert A. Harootyan. 1975. "Demography of the Aged." In Diana S. Woodruff and James E. Birren, eds. *Aging.* New York: D. Van Nostrand, pp. 31–69.

Dale, Edwin L. Jr. 1973. "The Young Pay for the Old." *New York Times Magazine* (January 14): 8ff.

Dales, Sophie R. 1975. *Benefits and Beneficiaries Under Public Employee Retirement Systems, Calendar Year 1974.* Research and Statistic Note No. 10-1975. Washington, D.C.: Office of Research and Statistics, Social Security Administration.

Donahue, Wilma; Harold L. Orbach; and Otto Pollak. 1960. "Retirement: The Emerging Social Pattern." In Clark Tibbitts, ed. *Handbook of Social Gerontology.* Chicago: The University of Chicago Press, pp. 330–406.

Epstein, Lenore A., and Janet H. Murray. 1967. *The Aged Population of the United States.* Office of Research and Statistics, Social Security Administration. Report No. 19. Washington, D.C.: U.S. Government Printing Office.

Federal Council on Aging. 1975. *Study of Interrelationships of Benefit Programs for the Elderly.* Appendix I: "Handbook of Federal Programs Benefiting Older Americans." Prepared for the Federal Council on Aging by the Human Resources and Income Security Project, The Urban Institute. Washington, D.C.: mimeographed.

Feldstein, Martin. 1974. "Social Security, Induced Retirement, and Aggregate Capital Accumulation." *Journal of Political Economy* 82 (September–October): 905–926.

———. 1975. "Toward a Reform of Social Security." *The Public Interest* 40 (Summer): 80–81.

Fox, Alan. 1974. *Earnings Replacement from Social Security and Private Pensions; Newly Entitled Beneficiaries, 1970.* Preliminary Findings from the Survey of New Beneficiaries, Report No. 13. Washington, D.C.: Office of Research and Statistics, U.S. Social Security Administration.

Friedman, Eugene A., and Harold L. Orbach. 1974. "Adjustment to Retirement." In Silvano Arieti, ed. *The Foundations of Psychiatry.* Vol. 1, *American Handbook of Psychiatry*, 2nd ed. New York: Basic Books, pp. 609–645.

Friedman, Milton. 1971. "Purchasing Power Bonds." *Newsweek* (April 12): 86.

Galbraith, John Kenneth. 1967. *The New Industrial State.* New York: New American Library.

Goldstein, Sydney. 1965. "Changing Income and Consumption Patterns of the Aged, 1950-1960." *Journal of Gerontology* 20 (October): 453–461.

Griffin, Frank L., and C.L. Trowbridge. 1969. *Status of Funding Under Private Pension Plans*. Homewood, Ill.: Irwin.

Hewitt, Edwin S. 1970. Testimony before the U.S. Senate Special Committee on Aging. In U.S. Senate Special Committee on Aging. *Economics of Aging: Toward a Full Share in Abundance*, Part 10B. Washington, D.C.: U.S. Government Printing Office.

Hodgens, Evan L. 1973. "Survivors' Pensions: An Emerging Employee Benefit." *Monthly Labor Review* 96 (July): 31–34.

———. 1975. "Key Changes in Major Pension Plans." *Monthly Labor Review* 98 (July): 22–27.

Hollester, Robinson G., and John L. Palmer. 1972. "The Impact of Inflation on the Poor." In Kenneth Boulding and M. Pfaff, eds. *Redistribution to the Rich and Poor: The Grants Economics of Income Distribution*. Belmont, Calif.: Wadsworth.

Kahne, Hilda. 1975. "Economic Perspectives on the Roles of Women in the American Economy." *The Journal of Economic Literature* 13 (December): 1249–1292.

Kreps, Juanita M. 1971. *Lifetime Allocation of Work and Income*. Durham, N.C.: Duke University Press.

Kreps, Juanita M., and Joseph J. Spengler. 1966. "The Leisure Component of Economic Growth." In National Commission on Technology, Automation, and Economic Progress. *Technology and the Economy*. Appendix 2: The Employment Impact of Technological Change. Washington, D.C.: U.S. Government Printing Office.

Loren, Eugene, and Thomas Barker. 1968. *Survivor Benefits*. Detroit: Michigan Health and Social Security Research Institute.

McGill, Dan M. 1975. *Fundamentals of Private Pensions*. 3rd ed. Homewood, Ill.: Irwin.

Mallan, Lucy B. 1975. "Young Widows and Their Children: A Comparative Report." *Social Security Bulletin* 38 (May): 3–21.

Maxwell, James A. 1975. "Characteristics of State and Local Trust Funds." In David J. Ott, Attiat F. Ott, James A. Maxwell, and J. Richard Aronson. *State-Local Finances in the Last Half of the 1970's*. Washington, D.C.: The American Enterprise Institute, pp. 35–62.

Meier, Elizabeth. 1975. "Over 65: Expectations and Realities of Work and Retirement." *Industrial Gerontology* (Spring): 95–109.

Mirer, Thad W. 1974. "The Distributional Impact of Inflation and Anti-inflation Policy." Discussion Paper 231-74. Madison,: Institute for Research on Poverty, University of Wisconsin-Madison.

Moeller, Charles. 1972. "The Role of Private Pension Plans in the Economy." In the Tax Foundation. *Financing Retirement: Public and Private*. Conference Proceedings. New York: The Tax Foundation, Inc.

Munnell, Alicia H. 1974. *The Impact of Social Security on Personal Saving*. Cambridge, Mass.: Ballinger.

Musgrave, Richard. 1968. "The Role of Social Insurance in an Overall Program for Social Welfare." In Bowen, et al. *The American System of Social Insurance*. New York: McGraw Hill.

Myers, Robert J. 1970. "Government and Pensions." In the American Enterprise Institute. *Private Pensions and the Public Interest*. Washington, D.C.: The American Enterprise Institute.

———. 1975a. Social Security. Homewood, Ill.: Irwin.

_____. 1975b. "Social Security and Private Pensions—Where Do We Go from Here?" *Industrial Gerontology* 2 (Spring): 158–163.

Nordhaus, W., and J. Tobin. 1973. "Is Growth Obsolete?" In National Bureau of Economic Research. *The Measurement of Economic and Social Performance*. New York: National Bureau, pp. 509–532.

Okonkwo, Ubadigbo. 1975. "Intragenerational Equity Under Social Security." Washington, D.C.: mimeographed.

Okun, Arthur. 1975. *Equality and Efficiency—The Big Trade-off*. Washington, D.C.: The Brookings Institution.

Orshansky, Mollie. 1974. *Federal Welfare Reform and the Economic Status of the Aged Poor*. Staff Paper No. 17. Washington, D.C.: Office of Research and Statistics, U.S. Social Security Administration.

Parnes, Herbert S., et al. 1974. *The Pre-retirement Years*. Vol. 4. Columbus,: Center for Human Resource Research, Ohio State University.

Pearl, William. 1976. "Mandatory Retirement at Age 65 Is Legal." *Pension World* 12 (January): 58.

Pechman, Joseph A.; Henry J. Aaron; and Michael K. Taussig. 1968. *Social Security: Perspectives for Reform*. Washington, D.C.: The Brookings Institution.

Quinn, Joseph F. 1975. "The Microeconomics of Early Retirement: A Cross-sectional View." Boston, Mass.: mimeographed.

Rejda, George E., and Richard J. Shepler. 1973. "The Impact of Zero Population Growth on the OASDHI Program." *The Journal of Risk and Insurance* 40 (September): 313–325.

Reno, Virginia. 1971. "Why Men Stop Working at or Before Age 65: Findings from the Survey of New Beneficiaries." *Social Security Bulletin* (June): 3–11.

Riley, Matilda White, and Anne Foner. 1968. *Aging and Society*, Vol. 1. New York: Russell Sage Foundation.

Rogers, John M. 1975. "Retired Couples' Budgets Updated to Autumn 1974." *Monthly Labor Review* 98 (October): 42–46.

Rosset, E. 1964. *Aging Process of Populations*. New York: Macmillan.

Ruggles, Nancy, and Richard Ruggles. Forthcoming. "The Anatomy of Earnings Behavior." In National Bureau of Economic Research. *The Economics of Well-Being*. Conference on Research in Income and Wealth. Vol. 41.

Samuelson, Paul. 1958. "An Exact Consumption-Loan Model of Interest With or Without the Social Contrivance of Money." *Journal of Political Economy* 66 (December): 467–482.

Schoeplein, Robert N. 1966. "Taxpayer Participation Under the Registered Retirement Savings Program." *Canadian Journal of Political Economy* 32 (May): 220–229.

Schulz, James H., and Guy Carrin. 1972. "The Role of Savings and Pension Systems in Maintaining Living Standards in Retirement." *Journal of Human Resources* 7 (Summer): 343–365.

Schulz, James; Guy Carrin; Hans Krupp; Manfred Peschke; Elliott Sclar; and J. Van Steenberge. 1974. *Providing Adequate Retirement Income —Pension Reform in the United States and Abroad*. Hanover, N.H.: New England Press for Brandeis University Press.

Sheppard, Harold L., and A. Harvey Belitsky. 1966. *The Job Hunt*. Baltimore, Md.: Johns Hopkins Press.

Siegfried, Charles A. 1970. "The Role of Private Pensions." In The American Enterprise Institute. *Private Pensions and the Public Interest.* Washington, D.C.: The American Enterprise Institute.

Slavick, Fred. 1966. *Compulsory and Flexible Retirement in the American Economy.* Ithaca, N.Y.: Cornell University Press.

Sobel, Irvin, and Richard C. Wilcock. 1963. "Job Placement Services for Older Workers in the United States." *International Labor Review* 88: 129–156.

Solow, Robert M. 1975. "The Intelligent Citizen's Guide to Inflation." *The Public Interest* 38 (Winter): 30–66.

Storey, James R. 1973. *Public Income Transfer Programs: The Incidence of Multiple Benefits and the Issues Raised by Their Receipt.* In Subcommittee on Fiscal Policy, U.S. Jt. Economic Committee. Studies in Public Welfare No. 1. Washington, D.C.: U.S. Government Printing Office.

Streib, Gordon F., and Clement J. Schneider, 1971. *Retirement· in American Society.* Ithaca, N.Y.: Cornell University Press.

Surrey, Stanley. 1973. *Pathways to Tax Reform—The Concept of Tax Expenditures.* Cambridge, Mass.: Harvard University Press.

Taggart, Robert. 1973. *The Labor Market Impacts of the Private Retirement System.* In U.S. Subcommittee on Fiscal Policy, U.S. Jt. Economic Committee. Studies in Public Welfare No. 11. Washington, D.C.: U.S. Government Printing Office.

Tax Foundation, Inc. 1969. *State and Local Employee Pension Systems.* New York: The Tax Foundation, Inc.

Thompson, Gayle B. 1975. "Blacks and Social Security Benefits: Trends, 1960-1973." *Social Security Bulletin* (April): 30–40.

Tilove, Robert. 1976. *Public Employee Pension Funds.* © Twentieth Century Fund. New York: Columbia University Press.

Torda, Theodore S. 1972. "The Impact of Inflation on the Elderly." *Federal Reserve Bank of Cleveland Monthly Review* (October–November): 3–19.

Trowbridge, Charles L. 1970. "Private Pension Funding and Vesting—Where Do They Stand Today?" In the American Enterprise Institute. *Private Pensions and the Public Interest.* Washington, D.C.: The American Enterprise Institute.

Turnbull, John G.; C. Arthur Williams, Jr.; and Earl F. Cheit. 1967. *Economic and Social Security*, 3rd ed. New York: Ronald Press.

U.S. Bureau of the Census. 1976. *Consumer Income.* Current Population Reports, Series P-60, No. 101. Washington, D.C.: U.S. Government Printing Office.

U.S. Bureau of Labor Statistics. 1966. *Retired Couple's Budget for a Moderate Living Standard.* Bulletin No. 1570-4. Washington, D.C.: U.S. Government Printing Office.

_____. 1967. *Three Standards of Living for an Urban Family of Four Persons.* Bulletin No. 1570-5. Washington, D.C.: U.S. Government Printing Office.

U.S. House Committee on Education and Labor. 1972. *Interim Staff Report of Activities of the Pension Study Task Force.* Washington, D.C.: U.S. Government Printing Office.

U.S. Dept. of HEW (Department of Health, Education, and Welfare). 1975. "1973-74 Nursing Home Survey—Provisional Data." National Center for Health Statistics. *Monthly Vital Statistics Report*. DHEW No. 75-1120, Vol. 23, No. 6 (Supplement).

U.S. Department of Labor. 1965. *The Older American Worker*. Washington, D.C.: The U.S. Department of Labor.

U.S. House Committee on Ways and Means. 1967. *President's Proposals for Revision in the Social Security System*. Hearings, Part 1. Washington, D.C.: U.S. Government Printing Office.

_____. 1967. *Social Security Amendments of 1967*. Report on H.R. 12080. Washington, D.C.: U.S. Government Printing Office.

U.S. Jt. Economic Committee. 1972. *Studies in Public Welfare*. Paper No. 2. Washington, D.C.: U.S. Government Printing Office.

U.S. Manpower Administration. 1970. *The Pre-retirement Years*. Vol. 1, Manpower Research Monograph No. 15. Washington, D.C.: U.S. Department of Labor.

U.S. Senate Finance Committee. 1975. *Report of the Panel on Social Security Financing*. Washington, D.C.: U.S. Government Printing Office.

U.S. Senate Special Committee on Aging. 1975. *Developments in Aging: 1974 and January–April 1975*. Washington, D.C.: U.S. Government Printing Office.

_____. 1970. *The Stake of Today's Workers in Retirement Security*. Washington, D.C.: U.S. Government Printing Office.

U.S. Subcommittee on Housing for the Elderly, U.S. Senate Special Committee on Aging. 1975. *Adequacy of Federal Response to Housing Needs of Older Americans*. Part 13. Washington, D.C.: U.S. Government Printing Office.

Viscusi, W. Kip, and Richard Zeckhauser. 1976. *Welfare of the Elderly*. New York: Wiley-Interscience.

Wallich, Henry. 1969. "Adjustable Bonds: Purchasing Power Bonds." *Newsweek* (November 24).

Weisbrod, Burton A., and W. Lee Hansen. 1968. "An Income-Net Worth Approach to Measuring Economic Welfare." *The American Economic Review* 58 (December): 1313–1329.

Wellington, H. H., and Ralph K. Winter, Jr. 1971. *The Unions and the Cities*. Washington, D.C.: The Brookings Institution.

Index

References to tables are printed in boldface type.

United States Supreme Court, 64, 99, 114
USSR, **5, 52**

Van Steenberge, J., xiii, 68, 71, 74, 78, 105–107
Vesting, 117–118, 130, 160, 165
Viscusi, Wikip, 87, 145
VISTA, 162
Vocational Rehabilitation Program, 161

Wales, **5, 52**
Walker, Charles, 78
Wall Street Journal, 136
Wallace, George, 133
Wallich, Henry, 77
War on Poverty, 25
Washington Post, 2
Wealth
  assets of aged, 21–25
  asset tests, 111
  auto ownership, **44**
  effects of inflation, 31
  financial assets, **76**
  home ownership, **44**
  prorated assets, 23
  statistics for aged, **24**
Weighted benefit formula, 95

Weisbrod, Burton A., 23
Weitz, Harry, 168
Welfare and Pension Plan Disclosure Act, 121
Wellington, H.H., 155
Western United States, 54
West Virginia, 154
1971 White House Conference on Aging, 102, 104, 145, 172
Widows, 16
Wilcock, Richard C., 55
Wilensky, Harold L., 87
Williams, C. Arthur, Jr., 87, 108
Williams, Senator Harrison, 164
Wilson, Thomas, 112
Windfall gains, 146, 149–150
Winter, Ralph K., Jr., 155
Work bonus, 151
Work/leisure trade-off, 46–50, 52
Workmen's Compensation Program, 161

Yugoslavia, **5, 52**

Zambia, 83
Zeckhauser, Richard, 87, 145
Zero Population Growth (ZPG), 6, 172